Performance Without
COMPROMISE!
"The Way Officiating Ought to Be"

A Tribute to Peter Webb

RAYMOND McCLURE

ISBN 978-1-64349-992-5 (paperback)
ISBN 978-1-64349-991-8 (digital)

Christian Faith Publishing, Inc.
832 Park Avenue
Meadville, PA 16335
www.christianfaithpublishing.com

Printed in the United States of America

"Officiating Basketball Games Is Not to Be
A Management Session by Artistic Philosophers."
Raymond B. McClure

Performance Without Compromise
By Raymond Boyd McClure

Rules Enforcement, Proper Mechanics, Approved Signals

Stop Managing and Officiate!

The Basketball Officiating Text Book
"The Way Officiating Ought to Be!"

Right-Way Lessons Learned From Peter Webb

All Commentary is Supported by the Rules Book and the Officials' Manual.

ACKNOWLEDGMENTS

My Best Friend and Wife, Susan "Susie" Cook McClure

Early one spring morning of 1987, Susie and I were sitting at the breakfast table each flipping through the *Atlanta Newspaper* when she said, "Here's something you'd like to do."

She handed me a classified newspaper ad that was promoting a summer camp for basketball Officials. It was like a bell rang in my head, and I immediately thought how "cool" it would be to wear an Official's shirt and blow a whistle.

Later that hot summer, I found myself in Carnesville, Georgia, at the Nationwide Referee Camp, which was run by Charlie Bloodworth and a few other veteran Officials. That was the beginning of a "love affair" that continues today. Susie has been the perfect wife during these many years of officiating, and I truly feel that every basketball Official should be so fortunate and blessed to have the same love and support that I have received from this amazing woman.

Thank you, Susie, for allowing me to participate in this avocation of officiating. Without you, I would have missed out on many friendships that have come my way through officiating basketball. Your support for my passion in officiating goes beyond measure, just like the love I have for you. Thank you for thinking of me while you were looking in the classifieds for yourself. You know I love you very much.

"He who finds a wife finds a good thing,
and obtains favor from the Lord"
(Proverbs 18:22).

My Friend and Mentor, Peter Webb

We had met previously, but I really got to know Peter Webb at a Jim Pepper/Ray McClure Officials Camp at the University of Georgia in 1999, as he accepted our invitation to serve as a camp clinician with us. That weekend would prove to be the beginning of our training as Officials together for many years to come and the beginning of a wonderful friendship. In addition, those many hours that summer proved to be a life-changing experience for me. The more I was around him, the more I realized I needed to do less talking and more listening. Peter has spent more time at the NFHS Rules Committee Meetings each spring than any other person in the history of basketball.

His insight and passion to basketball and basketball officiating is only exceeded by his love for his wife Marie, his family, his home state of Maine, and his love for country music. We have spent many nights in our travels, well beyond midnight, trying to remember the words of an old classic song while I endeavored to stay awake while strumming my guitar.

Thank you, Peter, for being an awesome mentor and instilling in me the importance of putting ***THE GAME*** ahead of myself or any situation. Thank you for allowing me to "hang out" with you, travel with you, and "pick your brain" at odd times of the day and night. But more importantly, thank you for being my friend and allowing me to be in the presence of the most knowledgeable person ever on the topic of basketball officiating.

Oswald Chambers is often quoted as he spoke of influence: "The people who have influenced us are those who have stood unconsciously for the right thing." That's you, Peter. Your commitment to **THE GAME** and why it's played in schools has never wavered. Yes, I have been "webbed," and **THE GAME** would be more accurately officiated had all Officials been so fortunate. You are a very special person, and please know this book would not exist without you and the influence you have had on me and my officiating. As others read this, they should know that they are hearing the same words I heard from you. Thank you so much for instilling in me that **THE GAME** comes first and all Officials should know that they can "trust the rules."

> "As iron sharpens iron, so a man sharp-
> ens the countenance of his friend"
> (Proverbs 27:17).

CONTENTS

FOREWORD

When asked by my friend and fellow basketball Official to write the foreword for his book, I began to reminisce of the many times we have shared not only for basketball officiating but also our love for classic country music and good Southern Gospel Music. We had much in common that led to many conversations in person and on the phone, many times at all hours of the night.

Raymond and I met in the late 1990s and in 1999, I was an invited guest at a summer officiating camp in Athens, Georgia, at the University of Georgia. For many years, he and I traveled to our country's military bases in Germany and Italy to train their Basketball Officials on behalf of IAABO, the International Association of Approved Basketball Officials.

During our time together, Raymond began to appreciate the same view of officiating I'd held for years. There is a right way and a wrong way, not a "mostly right way" to officiate **THE GAME** of basketball, especially at the high school level. I must say I have never had a better "student" than Raymond even after he was officiating college games. He has a tremendous respect for **THE GAME**, a determined attention to detail and a passion for officiating that is truly contagious.

Raymond has enjoyed over thirty years of officiating high school games, twenty-five years of college basketball, including twenty years at the DI level, three women's pro leagues, and currently serves as a Crew Chief and Rules Trainer for the American Basketball Association (ABA).

Raymond has also served on the Executive Committee for IAABO for several years, been a trainer for the Georgia High School Association (GHSA), and taught more than ten thousand Officials in his Basketball Officials Development Program.

It has been a goal of Raymond for many years to capture in book form the many lessons learned during the second half of his officiating career. I'm excited that he has reached that worthwhile goal, and this book should be read by all Officials, regardless of their experience level. This book is the accumulation of many years of research and more than four years of writing and rewriting. I am proud to say this entire book is rule based and manual based and is a pure example of how officiating should be.

As the reader, you will be amazed at the information you will glean from these pages. If you want to officiate the right way, by rule and not philosophy, I encourage you to read the entire book without skipping around. I know this book will make you a better Official, motivate and inspire you to constantly seek accuracy in your rulings, and have a better knowledge and understanding of the real role of the Basketball Game Official.

I can truly say I wish this compilation were available fifty years ago and was the training textbook for basketball Officials all across the United States and Canada. We believe in officiating "by the rules," and after reading *Performance Without Compromise*, we hope you will too.

Peter Webb
Maine Commissioner of Basketball
NFHS Hall of Fame
IAABO Past President

SOMETIMES A SINGLE
CONVERSATION
WITH THE RIGHT
PERSON CAN BE
MORE VALUABLE
THAN MANY YEARS OF STUDY.

Thank you, PETER WEBB!

**ALLOW YOURSELF TO BE
DRIVEN TO
EXCELLENCE IN OFFICIATING
BY AN ETHIC,
OBVIOUSLY SO RARE THAT FEW SEEK TO ADOPT IT.**

Thank you, PETER WEBB!

Why This Book?

"Accuracy Is Not Debatable."

This book is a *"call for commitment"* by Officials to a **Proper Performance** while making **Consistent, Accurate Rulings**. However, choosing a title that stated such seemed to take me about as long as writing it. I wanted a title that would instantly cause Basketball Officials to pick it up, thumb through it, and be so curious that they would not be able to put it down. I guess that's the goal of all writers of books. My motivation for this book comes from the fact that I have absolute genuine concern about **THE GAME**, and I have for a long time. My concern comes from my belief that officiating basketball is not as difficult as so many among us make it out to be. The truth is . . .

> **In my efforts to give back, as I am wrapping up a very long career, I cannot, in good conscious, pass on much of what I was taught.**

"*Much of what I was taught*" during the first half of my career had no rules support, was vague, came with poor advice, and even philosophical. Those clinicians and trainers were terrific individuals with a noble effort to teach me the "*right way*." However, there sure seemed to be many "*right ways*." Their training was also filled with too much about the "*tricks of the trade*" and not enough about "***the Trade***." I attended more than fifty summer camps after the age of forty, and sadly I report to you I was never instructed to trust the rules. Perhaps every camp director assumed the attendees were experts on the written rules, or they did not place rules knowledge as a top priority. Or, could it be, they never learned all the rules themselves and "got by just fine." Over the last four decades, we have become conditioned to accept less and less in the name of style, philosophy, and appearance. Less is not more; more is more. We must get all Officials committed to enforcing the rules, and they can't do that if they don't know them.

This book is long overdue because it is my attempt to . . .

> **Let the basketball world hear the words of Peter Webb, my mentor and the most knowledgeable person on the planet on the topic of "*basketball officiating.*"**

He would quickly and humbly deny this claim; but based on my personal knowledge of him and **THE GAME**, plus my fifteen years of serious research, I honestly believe it is an absolute statement of truth. When I got totally engaged in the International Association of Approved Basketball Officials (IAABO), it did not take very long for me to commit to a paradigm shift in my thinking and in my on-court performance.

> **This book is written to cause the same change in you, my fellow guardians of THE GAME.**

Each time you see a reference to **THE GAME**, it will be in all CAPS and **BOLD**. This is my way of constantly reminding each of us that **THE GAME** comes first and **THE GAME** is its rules. I do hope you will read it thoroughly, realizing that the author doesn't want to come across as a know-it-all but is a concerned Basketball Official who knows that after 126 years, we should not still be discussing what is an **Accurate Ruling** when we monitor Block/Charge, Continuous Motion, Traveling, Basket Interference, etc.

If you have been a Game Official for at least five years, you should be a **Rules Expert**. That doesn't mean you know it all, but it does mean you are in a comfort zone when you are officiating, knowing it will be a rare moment for something to happen during a game, which you cannot rule on accurately. Rules Experts know they probably don't know it all, but they sure want to, and that's why they are always a "student of **THE GAME**."

When speaking to a large group or just to the Officials in our Five-Star Course, I always ask them how long they have been officiating. Then I ask everyone who considers themselves a **Rules Expert** to raise their hands, and rarely does anyone raise their hand. This has bothered me for years, and still does. I am quick to inform them that I did not ask them if they "knew everything." There are thousands of Officials across America who actually do consider themselves as a Rules Expert. However, they are afraid to raise their hand because of the unfortunate and unfair question others all too often ask: "Yeah, but can he officiate?" Those who ask such a question are usually the more experienced Officials who officiate by the "seat of their pants" and have been doing so for many years. In addition, they obviously do not see the real value of officiating by the rules, which is required by the NFHS and NCAA. They prefer to "manage," instead of officiate. If they are not held accountable for accuracy, they can just continue to be accepted due to their Supervisor or Assignor simply stating, ***"Well, that's Joe's judgment."*** Let me be quick to say this, ***Joe's judgment has nothing to do with accuracy.*** You'll read it often in these pages, but if **Joe's judgment doesn't have rules support, Joe has been "*kicking rules*" for many years.**

It is well beyond high time for Basketball Officials to "*Join the Team*" and realize that we must stop making our task so difficult. Basketball, like all other games, is made up of Rules and Officials are to "monitor the activity and make rulings on that activity." Sometimes, the rulings have the sound of a whistle, but most of the time, the rulings do not need a whistle. All those Rulings must be supported by the Rules of **THE GAME** and Officials must stop trying to decide when to enforce them. As Peter has often rhetorically asked, with a hint of frustration in his voice, *"Don't these people know THE GAME has rules?"*

In addition, there is a required **Proper Performance**, which is defined and described very specifically in the Rules Book and the Officials Manual.

I hope you will enjoy *Performance Without Compromise* **but, more importantly, you will be motivated and inspired to honor THE GAME with accuracy and a proper performance and remove all substitutes for rules enforcement.**

By the way, please do not choose to disagree with what you read when what you read is supported by the Rules Book and Officials' Manual. If you do, then please keep reading, because I really want to *find the right words* that will convince you to not only *trust your partner* but to *trust the rules*.

WE FIND COMFORT AMONG THOSE
WHO AGREE WITH US AND GROWTH
AMONG THOSE WHO DON'T.
—FRANK CLARK

One More Thing

The Biggest Lesson Ever From Peter Webb

When we respect and honor **THE GAME** by enforcing its rules and officiating with the proper performance, as mandated by the Rules Book and Officials Manual, we are then performing our duties and role in a manner that is a *Performance Without Compromise*.

Officiating sports is never to be about you or me or what "we would do" in any given situation. Officiating is not about your opinion, your interpretation, your "feel," your tolerance level, your "call selection," or even your personal judgment. Officiating basketball games is about **THE GAME**, and **THE GAME** is its rules. You'll read it later, but let me say it here:

> *Nothing basketball Officials do is ever*
> *to be philosophical.* **Nothing!**

The Rules Book is not a novel any more than the Ten Commandments are suggestions. The Rules Book and the Officials Manual are the *blueprint* for accurate rulings and the required Proper Performance. Nowhere in the Rules Book or the Officials Manual can we find instructions to *do as we please* regarding Rules Enforcement, Proper Mechanics, and Approved Signals. **College supervisors and assignors of games seem to always hold their staff of Officials**

accountable for their appearance, their use of the organization's mechanics, their people skills (or lack of) regarding the coaches and table crew; but many leaders of Officials do not hold their staff accountable for Accurate Contact Rulings or the use of only Approved Signals. Why is that? The only reason I can *come up with is*, *they don't know the contact rules themselves.* If they did, they would not continue to categorize inaccurate rulings as *"Well, that's his judgment."* As stated previously,

> *An Official's judgment does not determine accuracy! The Rules Book determines accuracy! All judging is only accurate when it has written rules support.*

You will read many times in these pages the importance of *using only approved signals.* Think about it; one doesn't have to be a Rules Expert to signal as instructed by pictures in the back of the books. So when Officials choose not to comply, it is obviously an attitude of *"That's not important"* or *"That's my style."* This lack of compliance also demonstrates too many *leaders of Officials* feel the same way. When we all learn the reasons and the rationale behind every aspect of officiating, we are more likely to comply with the required performance as instructed in our Manuals.

As you are reading this compilation of officiating observations and explanations, the odds are, you will experience various emotions, perhaps excitement, when you *hear* what you've been wanting to hear for years or anger that anyone would have the *nerve* to say something like that, or you may feel an appreciation for this noble effort to get us all officiating by the rules, which is the only way we will finally all be on the elusive *same page.* Some of my remarks may cause you to think, *"That approach would never work in our area." "He's contradicting everything we've been taught."* Regardless of how you feel as you read these pages, I'll tell you the same thing I tell the trainees at our camps and at the Five-Star Basketball Referee Course we offer . . .

> *Everything you hear or read from me will have Rules Book support and/or manual support.*

You'll also quickly discover that my passion is strong and my dedication and devotion to **THE GAME** is unquestioned. **THE GAME** comes first! **THE GAME** is its rules! I hope you'll quickly realize that the purpose here is to persuade every reader to become a Rules Expert and buy into always demonstrating a *Performance Without Compromise*.

I am aware that college Head Coaches have an influence on college games and some of the material in this book may not appear to be useful or feasible to some college Officials. However, I do believe that every Head Coach, college and high school, would rather see their games officiated with consistent accurate rulings based on the rules rather than the Officials using some personal approach, personal tolerance level, some unique and personal "feel for **THE GAME**", or some organization's philosophy. Their games are presently officiated with "different officiating" nearly every night. Coaches at all levels should know what to expect because the Officials are all officiating by the rules and they are held accountable for their rulings. They should be held accountable for accuracy, not their personal judgment.

There are no new insights revealed among these pages; but this is a petition for all game Officials to know the rules, enforce the rules, remove all substitutes for rules enforcement, and perform the on-court duties as are so clearly described and defined in the Officials Manual and the Rules Book. I write not so much to inform the reader but to confront him/her with the necessity to *Trust the Rules*. Much study and preparation has been done over the last fifteen years by filtering through every known approach, philosophy, and *trick of the trade* that has ever been characterized as *training*. You will be presented with the best actions you can take to achieve consistent accurate rulings and do so with the proper performance.

Much of the history of basketball over the past four decades has been a history of "replacing substance with style" and with what sounded good to some person in authority who was never *really trained* at the beginning of their career. You can't make wrong work; we've been trying now for *who knows how long*. Accuracy is right even if everyone is against it, and inaccuracies are wrong even if everyone is for it. Accuracy does not cease to exist, because it is ignored, and it doesn't change depending upon whether it is believed by a majority. Accuracy is always the strongest argument. Accuracy is clearly stated. It exists. Inaccuracies are created. Accuracy needs no crutches. If it *limps*, it is inaccurate. It will *limp* without rules support.

Accuracy cannot be found outside the rules.

Unless everyone involved at all levels (Supervisors, Assignors, Officials, Coaches, Commissioners, Trainers) agree to believe in this mission of **consistent accurate rulings**, then we're going to be *wrestling the same bears* every year for the next 126 years, as we have done the first 126.

Each season we have Points of Emphasis (POE). Why? Because Officials are choosing to officiate *their way*, and not **THE WAY**, as instructed by the Rules Book and Officials Manual. One year the POE is hand checking; the next year it is verticality, then stop-the-clock signals, counting in the backcourt; and even one year, in both the NFHS and NCAA Men, it was *"enforce the rules as written."* It was shocking to me that Officials must be told to do this. There must be many Officials across the country who are choosing not to enforce certain rules until they show up in the front of Rules Book as Points of Emphasis. Why do Officials have to be forced to do what they are being paid to do?

We must find a way to hold all Officials accountable when they do not hold themselves accountable.

Again, if the Supervisors, the Assignors, and the coaches actually know the number of inaccurate rulings being made in their games, they will indeed be able to insist on **consistent, accurate rulings**. However, even if the Point of Emphasis is to **enforce the rules**, logic tells us, *"We can't make accurate rulings unless we know the rules."*

Stop *sugarcoating* your officiating, stop relying on your *feelings*, stop *preventing*, stop *play-calling*, stop *managing*, stop *controlling*, and stop officiating like you're a *weather vane*, changing to the way the *wind is blowing.* **Know and accept your real role** as a Basketball Game Official and accept it. Join the Team!

Not to be disrespectful but to demonstrate how too many Officials have a total disregard for performing their duties as prescribed in the Manual and the Rules Book, and conducting themselves as though they have been *anointed* to decide when and when not to enforce the rules of basketball, I submit the following *food for thought.*

If some Officials were soldiers in a war, they would have been shot as deserters. If they were doctors, they would be sued for malpractice. If they were lawyers, they would be disbarred.

JOIN THE TEAM!

Let everyone be sure that he is doing his very best, for then he will have the personal satisfaction of work well-done and won't need to compare himself with someone else.
—Galatians 6:4, TLB

**NATIONAL FEDERATION
OF STATE HIGH SCHOOL
ASSOCIATIONS**

NFHS MISSION STATEMENT

The National Federation of State High School Associations (NFHS) serves its members by providing leadership for the administration of education-based high school athletics and activities through the writing of **playing rules that emphasize health and safety, educational programs that develop leaders, and administrative support to increase participation opportunities and promote sportsmanship.**

CORE BELIEFS AND VALUES

<u>WE BELIEVE</u>...student participation in education based high school athletics and activities:	THE NFHS
• Is a privilege. • Enriches the educational experience. • Encourages academic achievement. • Promotes respect, integrity and sportsmanship. • Prepares for the future in a global community. • Develops leadership and life skills. • Fosters the inclusion of diverse populations.	• Serves as the national authority that **promotes and protects the defining values of education-based high school athletes** and activities in collaboration with it member state associations. • Serves as the national authority on competition rules while promoting fair play and seeking to minimize risk of injury for student participations in education-based high school athletics.

- Promotes healthy lifestyles and safe competition.
- Promotes healthy lifestyles and safe competition.
- Encourages positive school/community culture.
- Should be fun.

- Promotes lifelong health and safety values through participation.
- Develops and delivers impactful, innovative and engaging educational programs to serve the changing needs of State Associations, Administrators, Coaches, Directors, Officials, students and parents.
- Provides professional development opportunities for member State Association staffs.
- Promotes cooperation, collaboration and communication with and among State Associations.
- Collects and provides data analysis in order to allow its membership to make informed decisions.

"Always bring your high school officiating package to high school games."
HONOR THE GAME YOU ARE OFFICIATING!

 NATIONAL FEDERATION
OF STATE HIGH SCHOOL
ASSOCIATIONS

COACHES AND OFFICIALS CODE OF ETHICS

After thirty-one years of officiating basketball games, I am absolutely convinced that there is only a very small percentage of Basketball Coaches who have read or even familiar with Appendix F in the NFHS Rules Book. In addition, I am further convinced that too many Coaches could not *put their hands on* a Rules Book if asked to do so. In our Five-Star Course, we encourage the Officials to read the Coaches Code of Ethics—yes, the Coaches Code of Ethics. Since **THE GAME** is played for educational reasons, we strongly recommend that **Coaches be hired based on their acceptance to complying to every aspect of their Code of Ethics**. In addition, the following two Codes of Ethics should be taught during the initial training of Basketball Game Officials.

The **Officials Code of Ethics** is always located on the next page in the NFHS Rules Book at Appendix G. We normally read this one aloud in the classroom. Below is the Coaches Code of Ethics, followed by the Officials Code of Ethics.

COACHES CODE OF ETHICS
(From the NFHS Rules Book)

The function of a Coach is to educate students through participation in interscholastic competition. An interscholastic program should be designed to enhance academic achievement and should never interfere with opportunities for academic success. Each student should be treated with the utmost respect, and his or her welfare should be considered in decisions by the Coach at all times. Accordingly, the following guidelines for Coaches have been adopted by the NFHS Board of Directors.

- The Coach shall be aware that he or she has a tremendous influence, for either good or ill, on the education of the student and, thus, shall never place the value of winning above the value of instilling the highest ideals of character.
- The Coach shall uphold the honor and dignity of the profession. In all personal contact with Students, Officials, Athletic Directors, School Administrators, the State High School Athletic Association, the Media, and the Public, the Coach shall strive to set an example of the highest ethical and moral conduct.
- The Coach shall take an active role in the prevention of drug, alcohol and tobacco abuse.
- The Coach shall avoid the use of alcohol and tobacco products when in contact with players.
- The Coach shall promote the entire interscholastic program of the school and direct the program in harmony with the total school program.
- The Coach shall master the contest rules and shall teach them to his or her Team Members. The Coach shall not seek an advantage by circumvention of the spirit or letter of the rules.
- The Coach shall exert his or her influence to enhance sportsmanship by spectators, both directly and by working closely with Cheerleaders, Pep Club Sponsors, Booster Clubs, and Administrators.
- The Coach shall respect and support contest Officials. The Coach shall not indulge in conduct which would incite players, or spectators against the Officials. Public criticism of Officials or Players is unethical.
- The Coach shall meet and exchange cordial greetings to set the correct tone before and after the contest.
- The Coach shall not exert pressure on Faculty Members to give Students special considerations.
- The Coach shall not scout opponents by any means other than those adopted by the league and/or State High School Association.

 **NATIONAL FEDERATION
OF STATE HIGH SCHOOL
ASSOCIATIONS**

OFFICIALS' CODE OF ETHICS
(From the NFHS Rules Book)

Officials at an interscholastic athletic event are participants in the development of high school students. As such, they must exercise a high level of self-discipline, independence and responsibility. The purpose of this Code is to establish guidelines for ethical standards of conduct for all interscholastic Officials.

- Officials shall master both the rules of the game and the mechanics necessary to enforce the rules, and shall exercise authority in an impartial, firm and controlled manner.
- Officials shall work with each other and their state associations in a constructive and cooperative manner.
- Officials shall uphold the honor and dignity of the profession in all interaction with student-athletes, Coaches, Athletic Directors, School Administrators, colleagues, and the public.
- Officials shall prepare themselves both physically and mentally, shall dress neatly and appropriately, and shall comport themselves in a manner consistent with the high standards of the profession.
- Officials shall be punctual and professional in the fulfillment of all contractual obligations.
- Officials shall remain mindful that their conduct influences the respect that student-athletes, Coaches and the public hold for the profession.
- Officials shall, while enforcing the rules of play, remain aware of the inherent risk of injury that competition poses to student-athletes. Where appropriate, they shall inform

event management of conditions or situations that appear unreasonably hazardous.

- Officials shall take reasonable steps to educate themselves in the recognition of emergency conditions that might arise during the course of competition.
- Officials shall maintain an ethical approach while participating in forums, chat rooms and all forms of social media.

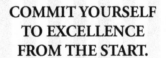

COMMIT YOURSELF
TO EXCELLENCE
FROM THE START.

CHAPTER 1

Accept Your New Identity

"You Are Now a Game Official.
Elevate Your Personal Standards of Quality."

Nearly all Basketball Officials were first players and perhaps even coaches in days gone by. That doesn't mean we all played on television at the Division I Level, but we probably enjoyed and even loved **THE GAME** as much as anyone. I recall running to the Physical Education Class at East High School in Rockford, Illinois, because I wanted to be the first one on the court so I could get some shots in before the bigger and taller guys got there; and they all were taller than my five-foot-eight skinny frame (still five feet eight but not so skinny). These taller kids dominated the rebounds, and all my future shots would come from my ability to run down loose balls.

Probably like you, I really enjoyed any amount of **THE GAME** I could get. Normally, I was the last kid to leave the gym because I felt it would be a *sin* to leave without making my last shot, which had to come from the top of the free throw semicircle, which would be a three-pointer these days by NFHS rules. Sometimes the first last shot would find *nothing but net*, but most of time I'd be all alone out there chasing the ball and returning to my *required shooting spot*, already wondering what acceptable excuse I could use for being tardy to my next class. I carried this same compulsive behavior on to Lee College,

Illinois State University, and men's leagues until I finally *graduated* to coaching my boys.

Many, if not most, Officials have never given any serious thought or consideration to the actual Role of Basketball Officials, as is discussed in a different chapter. It was not until my new friend **PETER WEBB** asked me the most thought-provoking question of my career, which was,

> *If basketball could speak, what would it say about the way you officiate?*

WOW! I had never even considered such an inquiry. This conversation led to discussions about Professionalism, Commitment, Loyalty, Dedication, and even Honor. Because of who Peter was, all I knew to do was listen as much as possible while making many written and mental notes. One of the first things he taught me was to *clean up my language.* No, he wasn't speaking of cursing or any form of vulgarity, because the Rev. Jack Andrew McClure, my Father, took care of that behavior issue many years previously. Peter kept educating me on the importance of *"accepting my new identity,"* which was that of an on-court Game Official. He would often remind me that,

> *"If you are going to be one, you should look like one and speak like one."*

Doctors have their own language; and so do lawyers, electricians, plumbers, professors, and all well-trained professionals, regardless of their chosen field of expertise. However, too many Basketball Officials want to continue speaking like the announcers, players, coaches, and fans. These are the same people that we often want to go into the stands and read them the Rules Book because their ignorance to the rules is the loudest noise in the gymnasium.

> So if they are so terribly uninformed, why do we want to speak like them?

We have our own **NEW IDENTITY**, and that is being *the highest-ranked person in the gym.*

We are game Officials, and we, too, have our own unique language, and it is found in the Rules Book and the Manual. So rise above that *"uninformed level"* of communicating.

It will take some effort and increased awareness to remove the *bad habit* of speaking like the *talking heads*, but once you do, you will never consider abandoning this initial all-important step of true basketball officiating professionalism. You will no longer refer to the End Line as a *"baseline"*; (there are no bases in basketball) or the Free Throw Lane as the *"paint."* Hopefully, you will be motivated to remove *foul shots* and replace them with the professional language of Free Throws. Below are a few others, which you will want to remember to change—that is, if you are *"buying into"* the importance of *speaking like a professional Basketball Official.*

PROFESSIONAL TERMINOLOGY VS. PLAYGROUND TALK

- **Screens vs. *"Picks"***
- **Division Line vs. *"Center Line"***
- **Free Throw vs. *"Foul Shot"***
- **Lane vs. *"Paint"***
- **End Line vs. *"Base Line"***
- **Throw-In vs. *"Inbounding the Ball"***
- **Basket vs. *"Bucket"***
- **Ring vs. *"Rim"***
- **Free Throw Line vs. *"Foul Line"***
- **No Shot vs. *"On the Floor"***
- **60-Second Time-Out vs. *"Full"* Time-Out**
- **Coaching Box vs. *"Coaches"* Box**
- **Score the Goal vs. *"Count the Basket"***
- **Officiate vs. *"Referee"* (Referee is a noun.)**
- **Rulings vs. *"Calls"***

There are others, but I'm sure you get the idea.

What if the surgeon were to say to his assistant during surgery, "Hey . . . pass me that sharp thing." Humorous, huh? We all could improve on that lack of professionalism by reminding the surgeon that the *sharp thing* is a scalpel. I encourage you to make the adjustment in this very important first step to becoming the professional **THE GAME** wants you to be; and . . . by the way . . . if anyone mocks you and conducts themselves as though this is not important, as has happened to me, pay them no attention, as they are not yet properly trained in this area of True Professionalism. Then simply remind them that **THE GAME** comes first and it deserves the **Honor**, which you are giving it. Often at games or camps, I have heard **PETER WEBB** quote Jesus with a smile, saying, ***"Father forgive them for they know not what they do."***

We are Game Officials. That's who we are. That's what we are. Man is the only creation that refuses to be what he is. Accept that identity. Our journey toward *"Excellence in Officiating"* begins with our commitment to using the language of the Rules Book. We judge others by their use of the English language. Uneducated individuals *"butcher"* the English language, and when we hear Officials *"butchering"* the language of the Rules Book, we can't help but suspect their foundational training as a basketball Official.

Our role is always too important for us to perform it at half speed, half-heartedly, half-professionally, and with an attitude that says, *"That doesn't matter."* To that we ask, *"Since it doesn't matter, why not perform as instructed by our instruction books? If it doesn't matter, why resist it? If it doesn't matter, then comply!"* By the way, **EVERYTHING MATTERS** more than most of us know, especially when you officiate for the right reasons!

> *"Carefully explore who you are and the work you have been given, and then sink yourself into it."*

Those who make fun of wisdom don't like to be corrected; they will not ask the wise for advice.
—Proverbs 15: 12

YOU CANNOT BECOME WHAT YOU'RE
DESTINED TO BE, BY REMAINING WHO YOU ARE.

CHAPTER **2**

Guardians of THE GAME

"So You Want to Be a Basketball Game Official?"

I decided to become a Basketball Official much later in life than most Officials. I went to college to be a coach and taught school one year in Peoria, Illinois, and then became an entrepreneur and have been ever since. Little did I know that being able to work *when I want and where I want* would allow me to officiate whenever I had the opportunity. One's family and occupation are two very important factors when choosing to become a **Guardian of THE GAME**.

I have met Officials who were as good as any Official needed to be to become a *TV Official.* However, their employment would allow them to only officiate close to home at high schools and perhaps local small college games. Others had small children, and being able to sleep in their own bed at night was much more important than building up points at Marriott. The ones who kept their priorities in the correct order proved to have a much better life in officiating than those who put this wonderful avocation ahead of their family.

Had I started officiating earlier in my life, I'm convinced I would have missed out on the cherished quality time with my children. God knows, even now, I wish I would have taken more time away from business and spent that time just *hanging out with them.* I am so thankful that I could coach my boys and watch my daughter cheer and compete in Roller Skating Events. Those days are gone now, but the memories are so very special. There is always a price to pay for success whether you are a truck driver who is gone most of the time or a local workaholic. However, I would encourage you, if possible, not to pay for that success in officiating with the hours you could be spending with those who will not be *"little ones"* very long.

I honestly believe I have attended more basketball officiating summer camps than anyone, over age forty, in the history of basketball. Since I did begin my career late in life, I conducted myself as if I had to *make up for lost time.* I literally started getting up an hour earlier every morning to study the Rules, Mechanics, and Signals in hopes of becoming a well-trained Basketball Official. I logically concluded that every Official was a Rules Expert, and I wanted to become one, as well. It made sense to me that Game Officials were officiating a game that had Rules.

All games have rules and participants are required to play by those rules. My *"job"* would be to know if they were actually playing by the rules; can't do that unless I know the rules myself.

Like many Officials in the south, my first officiating camp was the Nationwide Referee Camp in Carnesville, Georgia.

The Camp Directors were Charlie Bloodworth, Don Shea, Hank Nichols, Charlie McCarthy, Ralph Stout, and Joe Forte. The main thing I learned at my first camp was *how little I really knew* about a game I had played and coached for so many years.

Since that very hot summer of 1987, it has been a rare moment that I could be found without my Rules Book, Case Book, and Officials Manual. After a summer of studying, I could hardly wait to join a High School Association in my home city of Atlanta. Mr. Bloodworth, who would become a dear friend, suggested I join the Atlanta Area Basketball Officials Association. That made perfect sense to me, as I lived in the *Atlanta Area.* I would learn later that there were (still are) eight Georgia High School Associations, from which to choose in the Atlanta Metro Area. That was a long time ago, and I continue to ask myself, "Where did all the years go?"

Basketball Officials definitely are **the Guardians of THE GAME**. Coaches should accept that Role, as well. Even though Game Officials come in all *shapes and sizes*, various colors, younger and older, and both genders, the Role of Basketball Officials has, unfortunately, taken on a "different" definition than is intended by **THE GAME** of basketball. The real, true, and actual role is clearly defined in another chapter.

I am convinced that one of the *"great assassins"* in officiating is *haste*—the desire to reach your goal before the right time. Even though we all want to be on the *fast track*, it is crucial to realize that we should never try to rush the proper development of a game Official. Too many are seeking to be discovered before they are properly developed. It is very rare, in some states, that a new Official would ever officiate a Varsity game until his/her fifth season. **THE GAME** is the priority, and they do not want **THE GAME** to suffer due to an undeveloped Official.

> *"Too many younger Officials are like blossoms; if you pick the blossoms, you must do without the fruit."*

Officials should always have the courage to honor **THE GAME** enough to do what is right without thinking twice; they can't do that until they know *what is right*. Men and women who officiate are common; those who have really been trained are rare.

People with understanding want more knowledge, but fools just want more foolishness.
—Proverbs 15:14

RIGHT IS RIGHT AND
WRONG IS WRONG, AND
THINGS AREN'T NEARLY AS COMPLICATED AS WE
MAKE THEM OUT TO BE.

THERE IS
NO RIGHT WAY
TO DO
THE WRONG THING.

CHAPTER 3

THE GAME *Is Its Rules!*

"The Ten Rules Are Like the Ten Commandments; Neither Are Suggestions."

To make the statement, *there is contact in* **THE GAME** *of basketball,* is about as eye-opening as informing someone that fish get wet when they swim. One may think that Rule 4, where Definitions are listed alphabetically, would have Contact listed between Closely Guarded and Continuous Motion; but it is not defined there. However, the Rules Book is very clear that Contact does occur and unmistakably defines the two types of Contact as legal and illegal.

Illegal contact is defined as a foul, while legal contact is defined (NFHS Rule 4.27, NCAA Men Rule 4.21) as incidental; it is *just contact* that occurs due to there being ten players moving around in a confined space. The purpose here is to increase awareness that Officials can and should be seeking **Consistent, Accurate Contact Rulings**, instead of *anything else*. And to establish the fact that Officials can only know the difference between these two types of well-defined contact, if they know the Rules that apply to both types. As we are constantly reminding Officials . . .

> *You can't make accurate rulings, on rules you don't know.*

Since nearly everything players do is legal, we should be suspect that all contact could be incidental. As the covering Official monitors the *"before, during, and after"* of the contact, the ruling could remain as incidental, when no whistle is needed; or it could move beyond incidental into illegal, when a whistle is needed due to the foul. An Official who feels that the penalty is too severe has a right to feel that way; however, that Official does not have the right to set aside the rule.

Have you ever heard someone say, *"He doesn't know the rules, but he has good judgment?"* Okay, stop laughing; it is humorous. However, the truth is, **it is impossible to have accurate judgment without knowing how to judge**, since judging must be based on *something*, and that *something* is the Rules of **THE GAME.**

Doesn't everyone have the right to expect Officials to officiate by the Rules? Of course they do. This is a reasonable expectation, because when Officials don't officiate by the rules, regardless of the reason, inaccurate rulings are the end result. We recently heard of a crew of Officials who were reprimanded for misapplying a Team Control Rule during a throw-in. The bottom line is they *"kicked a rule."* But the good news is, they only *"kicked it"* once.

> **However, to my knowledge, Officials are never penalized or reprimanded for inaccurate contact rulings, such as inaccurate block-charge rulings, inaccurate continuous motion rulings, etc. Rulings on these contact situations occur many times a game.**

These Inaccurate Rulings are the same as *"kicking a rule."* If we knew we were going to be held accountable and reprimanded, would we find a way to stop *"kicking these rules"*? Too often we hear the leaders say, *"Well . . . that's his judgment,"* as if to imply that this Official never makes an Inaccurate Contact Ruling; he just has *"different judgment"* from, other Officials. However, when the same Official misses an out-of-bounds ruling, observers say things like, *"He sure kicked that one." "She was looking right at it and still missed it." "What was she thinking?"* Or as **PETER WEBB** would say, *"You've got to be kidding me?"*

But regarding Contact Rulings, we again hear, *"Well . . . that's her judgment,"* and the Official moves on to the next round in the tournament taking his/her *"Poor and Inaccurate Judging"* with him/her—many times affecting the final score, or even the winner of **THE GAMES** they officiate.

THE GAME of basketball is more than 126 years old, and during this time, we Officials have mastered many rules while failing to do so with others. For example, see how you do on these three true and false questions:

- **When the ball goes in the basket from above, points are scored. True or False?**
- **An out-of-bounds violation occurs when a player steps on a boundary line while holding or dribbling the ball. True or False?**
- **The free thrower can attempt free throws without being guarded. True or false?**

How did you do? My guess is you knew the correct response to be True on all three of these Case Plays. These are Rules we have mastered. Our judgment was very good on these three. But why were we able to judge accurately? Certainly not because of someone's personal approach or their unique judgment—but instead because we have learned these Rules. We have Rules support! We can provide proof!

> **It is time for us to accept the fact that the *"judgment of Officials"* is only accurate judging if we can support the judging with the rules of THE GAME.**

It may serve us well to know that there are only sixty-eight small pages in the NFHS Rules Book that contain the ten Rules of **THE GAME**, and they are very clearly written. So if they are clearly written, then Officials should be able to clearly understand them. If not now, why not? If not now, when?

It is becoming more evident that Officials and their leaders continue to approach **THE GAME**, as if Violations are to be *"judged by* *the rules,"* but contact is to be judged by *"something else."* However, if all the Rules are clearly written (they are) and Officials can learn to make Accurate Rulings that pertain to Violations, **they can also learn to make Accurate Rulings that pertain to contact.**

Contact should be ruled a foul because the Rules say so and for no other reason. It is time for all of us to realize and accept that the Rules pertaining to Contact are just as clearly written as those for Violations. The *"written word"* in Rule 10.7 is quite impressive, as it clearly informs the reader of what players can do and what they are prohibited from doing. Again, clearly written . . .

- what the Player can and cannot do . . .
- what the Dribbler can and cannot do . . .
- what the Shooter can and cannot do . . .
- what the Screener can and cannot do . . .
- what the Guard can and cannot do . . .
- what the Screened Player can and cannot do . . .
- what the Rebounder can and cannot do . . .
- and more . . . **IT'S ALL THERE!**

In fact, it would be very difficult to think of a contact situation in **THE GAME** that the Rules Committee hasn't already put in the Rules Book and/or the Case Book. It now appears that the governing bodies of basketball have *"seen enough"* and have come to realize that

> **The only way to achieve consistent, accurate rulings is to rid officiating of anything that is being used as a substitute for learning and enforcing the rules of THE GAME.**

However, Officials do not need to know the rules if their goal is anything but **consistent, accurate rulings**.

Recently, the NCAA Men only had one Point of Emphasis (POE): *"Enforce the Rules as Written."* For the same season, the NFHS's #1 POE was *"Enforce the Rules."* Since these were the POE, one would have to ascertain *"There must be a lot of Officials who are not enforcing the Rules of THE GAME."* We all should be asking, *"Why not?"*

The Officials Code of Ethics leaves us with no choice but to enforce the Rules of **THE GAMES** we officiate. So with this Code of Ethics and with this well-written Rules Book, we each should be asking, *"Why would high school and college Officials have to be told, after more than 125 years to enforce the Rules of THE GAME that integrity requires them to enforce?"* I'm sure we all know that integrity is certainly **not** the issue. Well then, what is the culprit? Why the mandate requiring Basketball Officials to enforce the rules?

> **Could it be that Officials are taught to** *"trust your partner"* **but never taught to** *"trust the rules"*?

PETER WEBB, retired IAABO Coordinator of Interpreters, was recently quoted as saying, *"As I tour the IAABO states and other states, we continue to see the same Inaccurate Rulings, year after year. We have many states that are not measuring up to the expectations of Basketball. IAABO—our Interpreters, Supervisors, Evaluators, Clinicians, and Officials—need to care about it all because it all matters!"*

One major general concern is the comingling of High School and Collegiate Rules, Mechanics, and Signals. This is unacceptable! Peter went on to remind us, *"The expectations of our high schools, as presented by the NFHS, is that Officials who serve them bring the appropriate High School Package of Rules and Officiating to their regular season and post season games."*

The Rules are very clear regarding what is legal and what is illegal for A1 and B1, as well as their teammates. However, as stated previously, Officials can't get rulings correct without correct Rules Knowledge. Officials and their leaders do not need to endeavor to *"figure out"* what is important or what does and does not matter. It all matters! Learn It . . . Recognize It . . . Enforce It. As long as we have Officials all across the land who *"take it upon themselves"* to determine what contact is legal and what contact is illegal instead of applying the Rules of **THE GAME**, we are not progressing, and games are filled with inaccurate rulings.

As stated in another chapter, Basketball Officials are the Guardians of **THE GAME** and much of what it stands for. We are charged with an awesome responsibility and . . .

> **Every time we walk out on the court, our goal cannot be consistency. Our goal should be consistent, accurate rulings, with the required proper performance.**

Basketball Officials are never to use *"substitutes"* for the Rules of **THE GAME**. We must officiate the *"Basketball Way"* . . . the right way. IAABO, the International Association of Approved Basketball Officials, has a Motto that has served its Officials very well since 1921: *"One Rule, One Interpretation."* Not only does this motto apply to Violations but also to Contact. The truth is, now that the Rules Book and the Case Book are so mature and clearly written, we probably don't need *"Interpretations."* What we do need is for High School Varsity Officials and College Officials to be Rules Experts before they *"graduate"* to that level of play.

Consistent, Accurate Contact Rulings can only occur when those rulings are measured by what can be proven in the Rules Book and Case Book. Leaders of Officials at all levels, whether they have ever officiated or not, must become very knowledgeable of the Rules so they will know when their Staff is or is not making Accurate Rulings, as opposed to just *"accepting each Official's personal judgment"* as good enough. Let's all accept the fact that *"Good Enough Is Not Good Enough!"*

> **Learn and enforce the rules. Accept the rules as the master plan, and by the way, many ask,** *"How long does it take us to learn them?"* **Hopefully . . . not another 126 years.**

Be perfectly joined together in the same
mind and in the same judgment.
—I Corinthians 1:10

"DEBUNK THE
NOTION THAT WE
OFFICIALS CAN'T BE NEARLY PERFECT."
—Peter Webb

CHAPTER 4

Four Training Topics To Learn First

"Learn These Foundational Officiating Topics Before The Rules."

Efforts to convince some Officials that **THE GAME** should be officiated the same in the 4th Quarter, as it was in the 1st Quarter, often falls on deaf ears. Too many of today's Officials have been influenced by other Officials and/or Supervisors, whom they hold in high esteem, and believe every word they say to be the *"gospel."* Some of these influential individuals are simply repeating what they have been taught by those who were never taught the Foundational Topics of this chapter. I once did the same.

These Four Foundational Training Topics are covered in this chapter, while the *"end of game officiating"* is found in a different chapter.

> **Officials will better understand and accept the *"right way"* to officiate near the end of THE GAME when they have been taught these foundational *"officiating 101"* topics.**

These very important Topics should be taught and learned before the Rules, Mechanics, and Signals:

1. **Why Schools Offer Basketball**
2. **THE GAME Is What Matters**
3. **The Real Role of High School Game Officials**
4. **The Importance of Rules and Rules Enforcement**

Without this **Foundational Training**, Officials cannot accurately and properly *"serve the cause,"* as expected by the NFHS and **THE GAME** of basketball. Without this **Foundational Training**, Officials get creative, mimic one another, and openly display a *"lack of trust"* for the rules of **THE GAME.** Without this **Foundational Training**, Officials easily *"buy into"* using substitutes for rules enforcement. Without this **Foundational Training,** *"end-of-game officiating"* will trade rules enforcement for a philosophy or some personal *"feel for **THE GAME.**"*

And . . . without this **Foundational Training**, the Officials will continue asking,

> *"Is this the time I enforce or not enforce that rule?"*

TOPIC #1: WHY SCHOOLS HAVE BASKETBALL

As stated elsewhere, and to further state the obvious, the purpose of our schools is to educate the children. We Officials and Coaches are to assist the schools in their purpose. Have you ever even thought of that? Has anyone ever taught this topic during your initial training as a Game Official?

> **When Officials accept games at the schoolboy and schoolgirl level, they are also accepting their role as part of the education process.**

Officials must realize that sports, music, and arts are part of the community and school's curriculum. Game Officials are major keys to ensuring that the intended life lessons are learned by the participating youth. These life lessons are the schools' main purpose of this extracurricular activity. When we Officials get this well established in our minds, we will stop inserting *"stuff"* into **THE GAME** that *"doesn't fit"* and has no place in the education process. Game Officials have a huge responsibility to the parents, the schools, and to **THE GAME** they represent. High School basketball is **not** to be officiated the same as college games. Why? Because these aren't college games!

See chapter 5 for the list of Life Lessons, which we refer to as *"Favorable Messages."* Many of these Life Lessons can only be learned outside the classroom. So you see, basketball is not played at the high school level for *"pictures of dead Presidents"*—meaning money.

Everyone involved in **THE GAME** must accept responsibility for assisting the student athletes in achieving these life lessons. Who is *"everyone involved"*? Well, that is a long list, as it takes many individuals to ensure that this extension-of-the-classroom event accomplishes its reason for existing. Here is a beginning list of *"Everyone Involved"*: Parents, Coaches, Media, School Administrators, Players, Spectators, Cheerleaders, Concessions, Mascots, and yes, Game Officials, etc. Of course, there are others involved, too many to list here.

> **Game Officials are in charge of THE GAME and shall not allow anyone to distract from the opportunity for these young athletes to receive these life lessons, which is the real reason for sports and other extracurricular activities.**

TOPIC #2: THE GAME IS WHAT MATTERS!

Every reader should easily recognize the *"real theme"* and motivation for this creation, which is the *"honoring of THE GAME,"* by placing it first and foremost above everything else or anyone else. No one and nothing is to come before **Accurate Rulings and the Proper**

Performance! It is easy to spot Game Officials who are dedicated and committed to **THE GAME**; they do not officiate in a manner or with a mind-set that is concerned with anything other than **Accurate Rulings and the Proper Performance.**

THE GAME is what matters, **Not the Coach!** Stop worrying about the coach, stop trying to please the coach, and stop selling your rulings to convince the Coach that *"you got it right."*

> **This is just as much of a distraction as trying to officiate with a rock in your shoe.**

Of course, this doesn't mean we don't need or use excellent people skills during **THE GAME**. However, it does mean that anything an Official does to win the approval of this emotionally charged and biased individual is a waste of time and a disservice to the schools and to **THE GAME.**

THE GAME is what matters, **Not the Players!** Stop being concerned with the number of fouls that a team or player has committed. Stop caring if they violate! Stop talking instead of enforcing! All of these concerns have been taught to Officials as their role, and **That Is Wrong!** This should be of no concern to us!

THE GAME is what matters, **Not the Fans!** Stop *"playing to the crowd."* Stop being a *"cheerleader."* Stop selling to convince them that you *"got it right."* Just do your job and get it right!

> **This approach hasn't worked. We've tried this for years. This is not our role. There is no Rules Book or manual support for being concerned with the number of fouls on anyone!**

When Officials demonstrate that they *"care"* about the Coach, the players, or the fans more than they care about **THE GAME,** others begin to ask themselves, *"Do the Officials care who wins?"* Solve these issues and make officiating much easier by removing such *"concerns and caring"* from your officiating. Putting **THE GAME** before anyone or anything else makes this change and our task much easier. Please don't *"cheat **THE GAME**."* Please don't leave it worse than you found it. It is over 125 years old. **Honor it. Respect it. Trust it. Protect it. Hold it in very high esteem.**

TOPIC # 3: THE REAL ROLE OF GAME OFFICIALS!

Another Foundational Topic that should be taught to all Officials is the **Role** of Game Officials—the **real** Role. If you are like most Basketball Officials, no one ever sat you down and spent 15–30 minutes teaching you the *"Real Role"* of Game Officials. What is interesting is the **Real Role** is clearly written in the Rules Book, the Officials Manual, and even in the Case Book? Those who are lacking on this topic will usually simply say, *"The main thing is to get the call right."* That is certainly a great start, but when only *"armed"* with this approach, Officials then start thinking that *"they got it right"* because they said it was right, their personal judgment.

> **These Officials should be reminded that nothing is about them. We are to be enforcers of the rules. If what we say . . . what we rule . . . is not supported by the written word, we just *"kicked a rule."***

Please read the above box again and internalize it! Again . . . nothing is to be about us.

I play in a couple of Senior Softball Leagues in Woodstock, Georgia, and last night (true story) while I was at bat, the pitch was obviously an illegal pitch due to the height being over twelve feet. The truth is, it was at least fourteen to fifteen feet high and would have easily passed over a basketball backboard. The rules require the umpire to signal for the defense and verbalize *"Illegal!"* so the batter knows he doesn't have to swing, since the pitch will be ruled a ball and not a strike.

The home plate umpire said nothing, and the ball landed on the mat strike zone. I said, *"That is an illegal pitch ump, way too high."* His reply was, *"I've been giving that high pitch to both teams."* My *"required"* reply then was, *"It is not about you or what you're giving. It is about the twelve-foot rule."*

The next pitch was no less than fifteen feet high, three feet beyond the rule, and I just stood there and turned to look at him, obviously taking the pitch. He said nothing. Luckily for me and the team, the ball did not land on the mat, which is the predetermined strike zone. That was ball four, but I stood there for about five seconds, which proved to be too long, as the umpire said, *"Careful Ray!"* I like an umpire with good people skills.

This is an excellent example of a Sports Official who does not put **THE GAME** on the high-esteem podium as we should. He has been trained that if he is consistent, it doesn't matter what he does. Proper, up-front **Foundational Training** will cause us all to never forget that **THE GAME** is **not** ever to be about us. Our **Role** is to *"monitor the activity and make accurate rulings based on that activity"*—not just any rulings . . . but **Accurate Rulings.** The accuracy is easily measured by simply comparing the Ruling with the written word. The goal can only be **Consistent, Accurate Rulings.**

TOPIC #4: RULES AND RULES ENFORCEMENT

The accuracy of rulings doesn't change. Accuracy is always accurate and *"selling"* an inaccurate ruling doesn't make it accurate. *"Selling"* demonstrates *"fear"* of what others might think. If the Official is okay with making an inaccurate ruling, as long as no one complains, that Official should . . . **Seek Help Immediately.**

If the main goal is to *"make someone believe"* you got it right, instead of actually getting it right . . . **Seek Help Immediately.**

If the goal is anything but **Accurate Rulings** . . . **Seek Help Immediately.**

As stated in another chapter, Game Officials are the **Guardians of THE GAME**, not the Coaches or the School Administrators. **THE GAME Officials!** We are the ones who hold everyone involved accountable to **THE GAME!** Accountability requires consistent, on-going accuracy!

> **The guardian is a keeper! The guardian cares! The guardian guards. The guardian is accountable to the schools, the parents, the community, and . . . THE GAME.**

- Coaches are to coach by the <u>rules.</u>
- Players are to play by the <u>rules.</u>
- Fans are to cheer within the <u>rules.</u>
- Officials are to officiate by the <u>rules.</u>

Get very serious about these **Foundational Topics of Officiating,** before concerning yourself with a pivot foot or Continuous Motion. As stated previously, without this **Foundational Training**, Officials cannot accurately and properly *"serve the cause"* as expected by the NFHS and **THE GAME** of basketball.

> *The truthful lip shall be established forever,*
> *but a lying tongue is but for a moment.*
> *—Proverbs 12:19*

BY WHAT STRANGE LAW
OF MIND IS IT, THAT AN
IDEA LONG-
OVERLOOKED, AND
TRODDEN UNDER FOOT
AS A USELESS STONE,
SUDDENLY SPARKLES
OUT IN NEW LIGHT AS A
DISCOVERED DIAMOND?

—Stone

CHAPTER **5**

The Role of High School Basketball Officials

"Ensure Life Lessons Are Learned."

I originally wanted the title of this chapter to be *The Role of Basketball Officials.* However, the role of College and Pro Game Officials is not the same as that of High School Basketball Officials. When High School Officials officiate the same as Officials for other levels of play, the schoolboys and schoolgirls miss out on the real purpose of sports within education.

The obvious purpose of schools is to educate the children. Schools sponsor sports and other extracurricular activities, like music and drama, because of the *"Additional Education"* received by the students when participating. This *"Additional Education"* is in the form of *"Favorable Messages"* the participants can receive because of their participation experiences.

Some, but certainly not all, of these very valuable life lessons and *"Favorable Messages"* are

- **Good Sportsmanship**
- **Fair Play Competition**
- **Learning to Follow Instructions**

- **Striving to Accomplish and Succeeding**
- **Learning to Lose Graciously and with Dignity**
- **Goal Setting**
- **Adhering to Standards**
- **Dress Codes**
- **Abiding by Rules**
- **Working Well with Others**
- **Teamwork**
- **Proper Group Conduct**
- **Acceptable Public Conduct**
- **Respect for Authority**
- **Controlling Emotions**
- **Discipline**
- **And many others . . .**

"Everyone Involved" in **THE GAME** of basketball should be working as a cohesive unit and accept responsibility for assisting the student athletes in achieving these *"Favorable Messages"*. These *"Favorable Messages"* must take priority over learning the individual skills of basketball and take priority over the attitude of *"winning at all cost."*

This responsibility does belong to *"Everyone Involved"* because these schoolboys and schoolgirls must receive top priority during these nonclassroom activities. When we think about *"Everyone Involved,"* we create a list that includes some very special people—individuals who always seem to have the children's *"best interest at heart"*: School Administrators, Teachers, Cafeteria Workers, Custodians, Parents, Coaches, Concession Stand Workers, Team Members, Mascots, Athletic Trainers, Media, Table Officials, and the on-court **Game Officials.**

"Everyone Involved" is responsible for maintaining certain standards and for maintaining the integrity of **THE GAME.** *"Everyone Involved"* must realize and accept the fact that Coaches and Officials are a vital part of the educational process. It is crucial that *"Everyone Involved"* understands that the Coaches and Officials are *"serving the schools"* in their respective roles. When there is a breakdown

in cooperation or negative criticism of one group by another . . . *"Everyone Involved"* loses, including **THE GAME** of basketball.

It is very much the duty and role of the Head Coach and Official to *"care about, monitor, and enforce rules"* pertaining to appearance, verbal and physical conduct, and sportsmanship in general. Sportsmanship is an expected priority for *"Everyone Involved."* The Coaches' Code of Ethics, the Officials; Code of Ethics, the Rules Book, and Officials Manual make this very clear to the Coaches and Officials of **THE GAME.**

Because of who we are, game Officials need to emphasize in early training what Officials are asked to do by basketball, whether others involved accept their role or not.

Kevin Merkle, an Assistant Director of the Minnesota High School League, had this to say on the subject, at the 2011 NASO Sports Officiating Summit in my home city of Atlanta.

"At the high school level, we're about educational athletics and educational activities, and we talk about that all the time and the values that Officials bring as they help to educate our young people and how important that is. And to take that proper attitude that you don't go into an event as an adversary to a Coach, but you're working with that Coach to provide a great educational experience for those kids. And having that proper attitude as you enter can make all the difference, as opposed to coming in like we're going to battle each other tonight. It's something that we're constantly working. I don't know if there's ever a magic answer to that, but I think we keep talking about that to try to build that belief in your Officials."

Again, there is a *"Big Picture,"* which is the purpose of this nonclassroom activity, and that is to have the student athlete receive and take away these many *"Favorable Messages"* from the experience of participating. Officials are representatives and *"Guardians"* of **THE GAME.** The major charge to these *"Guardians"* is the maintenance of standards, dignity, and integrity of **THE GAME** and its purpose.

Coaches and Officials should aid the schools in blending competitiveness, hard work, and the desire to win, with favorable and positive attitude and behavior. Coaches and Officials owe it to our young athletes to give them the proper guidance to help them learn these very important lifetime values in the form of *"Favorable Messages."*

Coaches and Officials must assume the responsibilities of being in a *"Role Model"* position. As Basketball Officials, it is our obligation to assist the schools in carrying out their mission statement.

High school basketball never needs to *"take a backseat"* to any games played at any other level.

In the perfect world, high school games should be the *"perfect model"* of how **THE GAME** is played, coached, and officiated. There have been thousands and thousands of more high school games played than college or pro games. If the NFHS (National Federation of High Schools) stopped all games until the college and pro games have played enough games to equal the number of already-played high school games, the next high school game would be played thirty-nine years from now.

Interscholastic Basketball really is *"The Big Leagues"* and should receive the honor and respect it has earned. This is where the aforementioned *"Life Lessons"* are learned while the skills are being enhanced. This is where the Coaches influence these athletes and demonstrate the behavior model needed to make good citizens, good employees, and good parents.

Why anyone associated with high school sports would want to change the high school rules to align them with college rules, instead of the other way around, is certainly not common sense.

It sure is easier to officiate, and it takes the pressure off when we passionately seek to make accurate rulings and simply commit to our well-defined Role as a High School Basketball Game Official.

A gentle answer will calm a person's anger,
but an unkind answer will cause more anger.
—Proverbs 15:1

**DON'T BE
REMEMBERED AS
A PERSON
WHO COULD HAVE
MADE A DIFFERENCE BUT DIDN'T.**

CHAPTER 6

The Real Big League

"Schoolboys and Schoolgirls Don't Play for
Pictures of Dead Presidents"
(Peter Webb).

As I indicated previously, my *"approach to officiating"* was totally changed during the summer between my tenth and eleventh season. I had five seasons of DI officiating *"under my belt"* and felt good about the progress I was making. Little did I know that during that Summer Camp at the University of Georgia, my entire officiating would take a huge paradigm shift, forever.

I recall being a good listener to my new acquaintance **PETER WEBB** as he would ask me thought-provoking questions that caused me to often say to myself, *"I have never thought about it like that."* Most of you would have been affected the same way. His way of challenging me without irritating me has served our relationship quite well over the years. He now doesn't try to *"sugarcoat"* anything with me, as he knows I listen when he speaks because I trust him to be the best *"guardian of THE GAME"* I have ever known. In fact, he is probably the *"best friend"* that Basketball Officiating has ever known.

Peter's background is in education; he served as a school principal for twenty-two years in northern Maine. So when discussions come up about **Why Schools Have Sports,** he certainly has much to offer on the topic.

Our personalities were, and still are, opposite of each other, as Peter is more *"laid back"* like the *"Wise Ole Owl"* and I am the aggressive one, who seemed to approach officiating with the *"ready-shoot-aim"* mentality. If someone told me something and I liked it, I'd be all in. I would add it to my officiating package without ever analyzing it or researching the Rules Book or Officials Manual for the proper justification for my new found *"trick of the trade"* or technique. If it were good enough for the guys on television with *"commas in their checks,"* it was certainly good enough for me.

However, as time went by and Peter continued to share *"golden officiating nuggets"* with me and do so in a nonconfrontational manner, I found myself and my entire *"approach to officiating"* had changed. The main thing that caused it was when I began to **Honor THE GAME** and **Care About Everything,** because, as Peter still teaches,

"Everything Matters."

Perhaps it was our mutual love for Classic Country Music that held us together initially. However, my continued desire to learn from *"the best officiating mind"* since Naismith still has me listening with both ears when he challenges my remarks on officiating basketball. It is a very rare moment when **PETER WEBB** shows how upset he really is, regarding the way some Officials perform their assigned tasks. I am always *"ready to write"* when he is speaking, and that preparation has proven to be a very inexpensive habit for me. It wasn't too long ago that I captured these words from him:

> *"Why Officials cannot accept the rules of THE GAME has always been way beyond my understanding!"*

He continued . . .
"When an Official accepts THE GAME assignment, he/she has an obligation to know and apply the rules at the level of THE

GAME being played. The NFHS rules are written with our youth in mind. Playing sports within the realm of high school education is very different than the levels of basketball beyond high school.

"Our nation's high schools want schoolboy and schoolgirl basketball to be an experience that our youth can apply to life: discipline, consequences for preparing well or not preparing well, penalties, rewards, adhering to rules, regulations, policy, procedures, etc. In all due respect to college and professional basketball, education and life lessons are not on their list of concerns.

"We leaders must continue to assist the Officials in understanding that they are not the rules writers, help them to accept that interscholastic sports are not like the NCAA or NBA. They are sports within education. Officials need to understand and accept their role and their role only. Learn the Rules of THE GAME and apply the Rules of THE GAME." Simply stated . . .

> *"Officiate THE GAME based upon the Rules and Allow the Rules Writers Who Are Representing the High Schools to Determine What Rules Are Best for the Purposes of Including Basketball Within Schools."* Basketball Officials are the highest-ranked people in the gym. We are there till the end of **THE GAME**, regardless of what happens. We have more authority than anyone. We outranked the Coach, the Priest, the Athletic Director, **THE GAME** Manager, and even the Policeman. We are **THE GAME** Officials! They can't play without us! In fact, without us, as we say at IAABO: *"It's just a pickup game."*

Once Basketball Officials internalize these facts, we can then get back to performing our assigned task as we are hired to do and stop concerning ourselves with the assigned tasks of others!

- **We are not the Coach, so stop coaching.**
- **We are not the Athletic Trainer, so leave the injured player alone.**
- **We are not the Official Scorer, so stop trying to keep up with their duties.**

- **We are not the Official Timer, so stop worrying about their responsibilities.**

In other words, since we already *"have our hands full,"* let's stay focused on our responsibilities.

> We have many Officials who are better at putting 2/10 of a second back on the clock than they are at knowing which foot is the pivot foot. We have a generation of Officials who are experts at what they are not asked to do by basketball but are not experts on the rules of THE GAME they are officiating.

Whoever tries to live right and be
loyal finds life, success, and honor.
—Proverbs 21:21

IT IS A WEAK MAN
THAT URGES AND
CONDONES
COMPROMISE.
EXCELLENCE IS
CONTAGIOUS, AND
WE NEED LEADERS TO START AN EPIDEMIC.

Attention State Associations/ Leaders of Officials

"There Really Is a Required Proper On-Court Performance."

"What is the proper performance for the basketball Officials in your state?" Respectfully, I rhetorically ask the state leaders the following questions:

- Is there actually a required on-court performance by your state's Basketball Game Officials? If so and they *"fail to perform"* as instructed, are they warned the first time or penalized without warning? Or could it be that your state doesn't have mandates regarding Mechanics and/or Signals? If not, surely every state *"requires"* their Basketball Officials to know the rules and enforce them.
- Does your state *"inspect what it expects"* and mandate certain exam scores?
- Are your exams an online open-book testing procedure? If so, does that provide you with sufficient confidence regarding their rules knowledge?

- Is your state okay with allowing their Officials to *"talk players out of fouls and violations,"* instead of enforcing the rules?
- Do you have closed-book testing to determine the rules knowledge of your Local Leaders?
- Do you have Summer Camp Attendance requirements?

It is nearly impossible to watch a JV game or a Varsity game anywhere, from any state, that would ever have both, or all three Officials, using the same Signals as they officiate **THE GAMES. Using NFHS Approved Signals are required by the NFHS Rules Book.** It sure seems obvious that we have really failed in this all-important area of nonverbal communicating. Perhaps some have failed to realize the importance of all Officials using the same Signals.

The missing ingredient in officiating is accountability, and we all know "when people are free to do as they please, they usually mimic one another."

When High School Basketball Officials are trained on the *"real reason"* schools offer sports (and drama, music, etc.), then it becomes easier for them to realize and accept that officiating high school sports should be *"nothing like"* officiating college or pro games; high school sports are education based, played for different reasons, an extension of the classroom.

The *"real reason"* these extracurricular activities are offered to students are the *"favorable messages"* that are to be learned by the participants. College and pro games are not played for these same reasons. **We should not want our Officials looking like and officiating like anything but high school Officials.** These games are much more important than **THE GAMES** that are played in college and pro. The Coaches and the Officials are to work together to ensure the student athletes learn the many life lessons that can't be learned in the classroom—lessons that will make them better citizens with socially acceptable behavior. This topic is well stated and in more detail in another chapter.

PERFORMANCE WITHOUT COMPROMISE!

> ## A basketball game is a basketball game.

High School basketball games should be officiated the same at every school in your state, the inner-city schools, the suburban schools, and the schools out in the rural areas. These schools play by the same NFHS Basketball Rules. The fact that some areas of the state may have better teams doesn't require a different officiating skill or some unique way to officiate **THE GAMES**. These more talented schools may require Officials with *"faster legs"* and Officials with **more experience at processing the quicker movement** of the players. And we recognize and know that the same contact that is a foul when the eighth grade girls' teams play is not the same contact that is always a foul when the more skilled, bigger, and stronger boys' teams play each other. Being able to recognize the difference is often what separates the quality Official from a *"whistle blower."*

> ## Signals are the language of Officials and a major component of the required performance.

Every state that uses NFHS Rules should insist their Officials use Signals from the NFHS Signals Chart since those are the **Signals** that are required by the **NFHS** rules. Signaling is a vital part of the required Proper Officiating Performance, and when the local State Basketball Officials are not held accountable, they just do whatever they want and mimic one another. Some want to look like college Officials, and others desire to emulate NBA Officials. High School Organization leaders should *"pride themselves"* in using Officials who *"pride themselves"* in their performance for the State Association.

So where does that leave us? We really want to see each state hold their Officials accountable and provide them with training that would motivate and inspire them to improve the performance of their on-court Officials. Why have the Officials been so eager to copy a style and yet so reluctant to copy the Officials Manual? Are they interested in looking like something they are not? Do any college Officials try to look like high school Officials during their college games? State Association leaders should mandate that all their Officials accept their identity as a High School Game Official. And . . . *"find a way"* to motivate their Officials to demonstrate pride, professionalism, and poise as they officiate games that are played for a greater reason than money—the aforementioned *"Life Lessons."*

What is holding your state back from requiring your Officials to simply start signaling like high school Officials are supposed to signal and stop condoning unapproved signaling?

Do our State Leaders think that signaling is no big deal? Is their attitude one that states, *"The main thing is to get the call right?"* Have they even considered the NFHS Signals Chart?

Some High School Officials, who also officiate college games, are constantly trying to do something during their high school games that will be a *"clue to others"* that they are *"really a college Official"* and this game is *"so fortunate to have them in it."* We have now reached the point in this deterioration process that these same Officials, who officiate high school and college games, are now wanting to *"look even more like college Officials than ever before."* They are standing like college Officials, signaling like college Officials and trying to *"manage a game"* like college Officials and failing to realize that **THE GAME** is not played for the same reasons in high school as they are in college gyms.

When polling High School Head Coaches, we learned that they will be the first to tell us that they prefer quality High School Officials over quality College Officials. Each state has more of the former than the latter and those Officials are the ones who are dedicated to their state association, not the Officials who only officiate high school games when they have an open date. Post-season games should be the reward for a *"job well done"* and a *"thank-you"* for the commitment to the state high school association. That reward should not go to college Officials who only officiate enough games to be qualified to take the reward from qualified high school Officials who have served in twice as many games for the state association during the regular season.

Does your state really *"inspect what you expect"*?

Many Officials have been hired or promoted because of how they look in a uniform, how they run, and how wide they can spread their fingers when reporting fouls. These may be desirable traits, but they cannot and should not take precedence over Rules Knowledge. Without the proper training that should come first, these untrained Officials will look good on the court, but their officiating will contain inaccurate rulings, and **THE GAME** deserves better. Not knowing the rules, not enforcing the rules, and trying to manage **THE GAME** by using substitutes for Rules Enforcement, instead of officiating **THE GAME** as required by its rules, should no longer be condoned. To state the obvious, ***"We can't make accurate rulings if we don't know the rules."***

Our Role, as a Game Official, is to ***"monitor the activity and make accurate rulings on that activity."*** If our rulings do not have rules support, they are not accurate, regardless of how well we *"sell"* them. *"Selling"* inaccurate rulings will never make them accurate. This lack of rules knowledge seems to be a disease among Officials— actually an epidemic—that continues to spread across the entire country. It really is shocking as to the number of times each season that I am contacted to clarify a rule that should have been learned the first week before ever going onto the court. However, the real *"shocker"* is who is doing the asking.

Are your Officials who have at least five years' experience rules experts?

If not, why not? If your state uses an open-book or an online exam each year to determine the rules knowledge of your Officials, let me encourage you to rethink that type of testing and consider using *"real"* testing with a closed Rules Book and a Proctor for the exam.

If your state doesn't have summer camp requirements, perhaps you should consider offering them and motivate your Officials to commit to continuing education in officiating. If your state does have required summer camps, who serves as Clinicians at your camps? All too often, our Camps get college Officials to serve as Clinicians. Too many of which haven't been on a high school court in years. The only way these individuals know how to train is the way they currently officiate in college games. Again, they are probably proficient at officiating games that are played for different reasons than high school games, and so their officiating is **not the same** as it should be at the high school level.

> **Different rules. Different mechanics. Different signals.**

They are training our High School Officials using philosophies, management techniques, tricks of the trade, and substitutes for rules enforcement. **There is no place in high school basketball games for such training.** This game is now over 125 years old, and we cannot continue to condone our Officials as they try to decide *"when to enforce certain rules."* Philosophies teach and allow Officials to decide for themselves when they should sound the whistle, is this the right moment? The right score? The right situation?

One Clinician tells them, ***"You should not have called that, since there is only eighteen seconds to go in THE GAME."*** Another Clinician tells them, ***"You should have called that since there's only eighteen seconds to go in THE GAME."*** Again, high school games don't need someone's philosophy. *"We have Rules!"* These rules are **THE GAME.** These Rules are to be honored. These Rules have been created, modified, enhanced, and rewritten for over 126 years; and **they are now very clear.** It is high time for State and Local Leaders to **only condone Accurate Rulings and a Proper Performance.** However, unless the State and Local Leaders are Rules Experts themselves, they will *"not really know the accuracy"* of the rulings by their Officials.

All of this has led to no accountability for **Signaling**, so they do as they please. All of this has led to no accountability for inaccurate rulings and dismissed as, *"Well that's his judgment."* If his judgment has no rules support, he just *"kicked a rule"* and affected the final score and, in some cases, even affected which team won and which team lost.

My very educated guess is, when your state has more *"game managers"* and philosophers who have replaced **Game Officials**, the more fights you'll have. Could fighting at schoolboy and schoolgirl games be due to Officials *"warning for bad behavior"* instead of a **Zero Tolerance** for unsporting behavior? Do Officials know that players will *"seek and find"* their own **revenge** for painful illegal contact that is not ruled to be a foul? Do Officials know that their whistle often serves as the **Revenge** for the illegally contacted player? No number of warnings will provide such **revenge.**

> **Some state tournament Officials are an embarrassment to schoolboy and schoolgirl basketball.**

They do not **Honor THE GAME**, they do not **trust their partners**, and rarely do they ever signal properly using only **Approved NFHS Signals**. They are allowed to *"do as they please,"* and their improper performance is condoned by Leaders and then copied by their peers.

> **We are high school Officials who officiate high school games. Is there anything wrong with being and looking like *"who we are"*?**

Does your state condone the following lack of rules enforcement? Does your state condone unapproved signals? These are the **rules** that were too often **not enforced** during the State Finals last year in a few states we observed, along with commentary regarding styles and signaling.

RULES NOT ENFORCED

- **Rule 10.6.1.a . . . Coaching Box** (almost totally ignored)
- **Rule 4.10 and Rule 9.10.1.a . . . Closely Guarded** (Either they don't know six feet, or they want to avoid having a violation; when they do count, it is nearly always at half speed.)

- **Rule 2.7.9 . . . 10-Second Backcourt Count** (often no count; when they do count, it is often at half speed.)
- **Rule 2.7.9 . . . Throw-In Count** (speeds vary . . . Never too fast but often at half speed)
- **Rule 2.7.9 . . . Wrist Flick on Free Throws** (sometimes no count; often at half speed)
- **Rule 10.4.3 . . . Grasping the Basket** (grasping is a technical foul; exception: to avoid injury to self or others; most times injury is not a possibility.)
- **Rule 4.23 . . . Guarding/Block/Charge (THEY JUST DO NOT KNOW THIS RULE)**
- **Rule 4.44 . . . Traveling** (changing pivot foot: no whistle; stepping after jump stop: no whistle; illegal spin move: no whistle)
- **Rule 4.11 . . . Continuous Motion** (Too often Officials penalize the *"good guy"* who is the one who has already begun the *"act of shooting."*)

UNAPPROVED SIGNALS

- Fist to Start Clock **(FIST IS FOR FOULS** regardless of how it is done other places.)
- NBA Three-Point Signal (Full Hand, Not 3 FINGERS AT HEAD LEVEL)
- Directional Signal (One Finger, Instead of Four Fingers)
- Team Control Foul Signal . . . ***"Offense"!*** (Instead of Player Control Signal)
- Rule 2.9 . . . Site of Foul or Violation (We have created *"hit-and-run"* Officials: *"hit the whistle and run to the table."*)

STYLE VS. SUBSTANCE

Too often, Officials seem to be saying, *"Look at me closely and you'll see I'm really a college Official."*

- **Free Throws**
  - o Often they have no whistle in their mouth on the first free throw while the ball is live with rules to enforce and points at stake.
  - o Often appearing disinterested in monitoring the players
  - o Hands on hips while looking around the gym with whistle hanging out of mouth instead of monitoring the players and their activity.
  - o Often no ten-second count. When they do count . . . **way** too slowly.
  - o Standing on the nearest lane line until the last free throw
- **Warnings, Warnings, and More Warnings, Pertaining to . . .**
  - o Coaching Box
  - o Shirt Tails and Rolled-Down Shorts
  - o Unsporting Behavior
    - ▪ Head Coaches
    - ▪ Players
    - ▪ Bench Personnel
- **Game Managers Instead of Game Officials**
  - o Talking Instead of Enforcing
    - ▪ *"Get your hands off!"*
    - ▪ *"Get out of the lane!"*
    - ▪ *"Get off one another!"*
  - o Using substitutes for rules enforcement
  - o Don't consider both teams
  - o Trying to keep the foul counts even
  - o Trying to keep the star player in THE GAME
  - o Knowing the problem player and he/she gets no warnings
  - o Some don't even use a lanyard while trying to look like an NBA Official.
  - o Standing with whistle in hand during half-court offense, causing too long of a delay when whistle is needed for foul or violation.

More Questions . . .

- Do you really know when your Officials make inaccurate rulings pertaining to Block/Charge, Continuous Motion, Basket Interference, Over and Back, and Traveling?
- Do you really know that your Officials can't have good judgment if they don't know the rules?
- Do you accept the fact that high school extracurricular activities are an extension of the classroom and are education-based?
- Do you believe high school basketball is played for different reasons than college or Pro games?
- Do you think that most fights in basketball games could have been prevented?
- How many fight reports did your state office received this past season?

I hope this chapter has increased your awareness of the lack of **Consistent Proper Performances** and a lack of **Accurate Rules Enforcement** in high school games in nearly every state. I further hope that if you know anyone who condones such officiating that you'll join with me in seeking to get them to **Join the High School Officiating Team.**

If we can get all high school camps training high school Officials, the high school way, which really is the **Basketball Way**, perhaps eventually the fans and coaches, and even our fellow Officials, will start seeing the same accurate rulings each and every game. The Coaches' Code of Ethics and the Officials' Code of Ethics make it very clear that we certainly must at least try. This is a call to action for *"leaders of Officials"* (State Directors, Assigners, Supervisors, etc.) to **stop putting your approval on inaccurate rulings. Stop putting your approval on substitutes for rules enforcement. Stop putting your approval on a poor on-court performance.**

Please help Officials who have been officiating for ten years to actually have ten years' experience instead of one-year experience ten times.

Be sure that no one leads you away
with false and empty teaching . . .
—Colossians 2:8

THE GAME ITSELF IS THE ENTERTAINMENT.
THE GAME IS ITS RULES. TO OFFICIATE
WITHOUT ENFORCING THEM IS INSULTING.
"IF I WANT THAT TYPE OF ENTERTAINMENT,
I'LL GO WATCH THE GLOBETROTTERS."

—John Wooden

CHAPTER 8

NFHS Officials' Quarterly 2001 Article

"An Older Article Titled 'Rules or Mechanics, Choose Both.'"

For many years, I have been trying to get Officials to pridefully officiate the *"right way,"* and there really is a *"right way."* The article below was published back in the summer of 2001 in the *NFHS Officials' Quarterly*. That proved to be the beginning of some concerted efforts to get Officials to demonstrate a *"Performance Without Compromise."* Since this article, I have replaced the word *"call"* with the verb *"rule"* and the noun *"Referee"* with *"Official,"* since there is only one R in each game. In addition, *"referee"* is not a verb, but *"officiate"* is. In other words, *"Referees don't referee,"* but *"Officials do officiate."* This really does more accurately describe the role of game Officials.

As you already know, we believe Officials should speak like the professionals we are, using **Rules Book terminology**. Still today, many years since the publishing of the article, we still have Officials who perform their on-court duties with an attitude of *"The main thing is to get the call right,"* as if they must choose between accuracy and the proper performance.

Before I continue typing and rewriting the article, I'll stop here so you can read it as it was written and published back in 2001.

RULES OR MECHANICS CHOOSE BOTH

Ray McClure

Our goal in officiating is to have our Officials call **THE GAMES** by interpreting the rules and mechanics the same way. Obviously, the intent is to have the Officials make the rulings the same, therefore never *"kicking"* a rule. This is, without a doubt, a must! The Officials absolutely must get the calls right.

So again, our goal is **PERFECTION** in the knowledge and interpretation of the rules by **ALL OFFICIALS.** This can only be accomplished by each and every Official studying and learning the rules from the *"one and only"* Rules Book available, with additional studies from the Case Book and the Simplified and Illustrated book. These are the only books that are available to all Officials nationwide. There are other excellent materials, clinics and camps, but again, only these nationally published materials are available to each and every Official. So . . . **CONSISTENCY** in *"whistleblowing"* is only obtained by all Officials having complete knowledge of and enforcing the same rules **THE SAME WAY.** This is the best way to *"sell calls"*: to make sure the *"price"* is always the same.

Have you ever heard anyone make the statement: *"He doesn't know the rules, but he sure has great judgment."*? This is, without a doubt, a statement of pure ignorance. It is literally impossible for anyone to *"make proper and accurate rulings"* on rules they don't know! After all, this is what we do: **Make rulings.** Isn't that true?

Whether the Official does a good job or a bad job of enforcing the rules of **THE GAME** has nothing to do with whether he/she uses proper signals and mechanics, with one exception: it has been proven, and accepted by all, that when the Official uses the proper floor positions and calls in his/her primary coverage area, he/she will get a *"better look,"* and the accuracy of the calls improves greatly. But whether the Official points and counts with the proper hand, bird dogs or not, gives the approved signal or reports to the table in the reporting area does nothing to improve the accuracy of the calls.

So . . . rules knowledge and the interpretations of these rules are **NOT DEPENDENT** on the use of proper mechanics and signals. Therefore, Officials must understand that it is not necessary to choose between rules knowledge and using proper mechanics and signals. These are two totally separate components of officiating **THE GAME**. It is very possible for an Official to be knowledgeable in the rules, but poor in the mechanics and signals. It is also very possible for an Official to use proper mechanics and approved signals, but not have the knowledge of the rules needed to pass a test or to officiate **THE GAME** with accuracy. There is also the possibility that some Officials will become experts in both these areas, but for other reasons, still not become very good Officials. That does not, however, change the fact that these two separate components are the foundation on which the good Official is built.

Since it is not necessary to make a choice between rules and mechanics and signals, the response to the importance of using proper mechanics and approved signals does not need to be: *"It's more important to get the calls right!"*

Even though that should *"go without saying,"* it is no doubt an effort to disguise the obvious: The Official has not taken the time nor put in the necessary effort to learn the *"art of presenting"* the entire *"package"* properly. Or, he/she has not been required by the assignor or supervisor to become proficient in this area. In some states, all that is required to become an Official is to purchase a referee shirt and a whistle. The new Official is put on the floor to learn *"as he goes."* What is even more disturbing is the Official is sometimes perceived as competent, and advances, based on his/her appearance and style. This is an injustice to the Official, his/her peers and **THE GAME** he/she officiates.

If you were to go to your favorite restaurant and order your favorite steak and they prepared it to your exact specifications, and then they served it to you sizzling on a garbage can lid, it would probably lose its appeal, and you might even refuse to accept the steak altogether, unless the server really did a great sales job on you.

Don't forget, the steak was prepared **EXACTLY** as you ordered it. The problem was not the steak; the problem was the presentation. But remember, you did not order or specify a certain presentation; you just expected it. You expected the quality of the presentation to be as appealing as your steak. You expected the presentation to be the same as it has been in the past from other servers. What a *"surprise"* to occur at your favorite restaurant.

When you go shopping for that special piece of jewelry, you can count on a nice presentation at the jewelry store. The sales clerk is careful to present the diamond ring or bracelet on a beautiful velvet background. But, what if the clerk were to present this expensive and beautiful piece of jewelry by simply laying the item on the glass counter or, even worse, on a piece of cardboard or old newspaper? Wouldn't this presentation be lacking? Isn't it true, that without the proper presentation, this special moment would somehow not be the same? Isn't it also true, however, that the presentation in no way modifies the quality of the merchandise? Just the quality of the moment! These examples demonstrate the two necessary components needed to make the sale and have a satisfied customer. Neither the restaurant nor the jewelry store had to choose between the quality of their merchandise and the quality of their presentation, **BUT THEY DID!**

There are too many Officials today who are being promoted or rewarded before developing the *"complete package."* Once again, for Officials to advance to the next level too soon is doing the Official and **THE GAME** we serve a very serious disservice. There are some supervisors and assignors who have failed to require the Official to learn and develop these all-important ingredients necessary to be the *"complete Official."* One cannot fault the Official for accepting the advancements. But, those of us involved in the training of Officials would encourage those responsible for promotions to keep these incompetent whistle-blowers from sending the message to our trainees that it is not necessary to attend the camps and other forms of continuing education in order to advance. It seems that in lieu of training the Official, too much emphasis has been placed on learning the *"art of selling"* and developing a certain look or style. Officials are encouraged to develop their own style, as long as it does not contradict the Manual. However, when Officials are not held accountable for their poor mechanics/signals performance, they receive the message that what they are doing is acceptable, and therefore no change is necessary, and bad habits are formed that appear to be permanent. If all Officials were using the same mechanics and signals, the coaches would be seeing the same presentation every game. No surprises, no expectations, no selling required, no refs being head cheerleaders, no emotional and excited Officials. Just the same presentation from the Official who has the *"complete package"* every game!

Remember the above article was published in 2001.

If I were to submit the same article in the present day, it would have several changes due to my acceptance and commitment to honoring **THE GAME** with even more professional Rules Book terminology. Since 2001, when the above article was published, it bothers me to say the on-court performance of TV Officials is even worse, as they continue to *"do as they please"* and continue to use *"substitutes"* for rules enforcement. If you are a supervisor, an assignor, or trainer of Officials, please become a rules expert yourself because you'll then be able to hold your staff of Officials accountable for all their rulings, including contact, and not *"brush it off"* by saying, *"Well that's his judgment."* If *"his judgment"* has no rules support, his *"judging"* is filled with ***"inaccurate rulings."***

> ***A healthy tree cannot bring forth bad fruit,***
> ***neither can a poor tree bring forth good fruit.***
> ***—Jesus, Matthew 7:18***

THE FURTHER A
SOCIETY DRIFTS FROM
THE TRUTH,
THE MORE IT WILL HATE THOSE WHO
SPEAK IT.

—George Orwell

CHAPTER 9

NFHS Officials' Quarterly, 2004 Article

"Prisoners of Damaging Misconceptions"

This chapter is another NFHS Article, which I submitted and was published in 2004, where we were making a serious effort to increase awareness of the many *"contradictions to the rules"* that were being taught as the *"gospel."* Remember, in 2004, I was in my thirteenth season of officiating DI Men's basketball games and four years since I had been *"webbed"* by **PETER WEBB**, the best basketball-officiating mind I have ever met. Too much of the *"training"* we were seeing, and too much of the magazine articles we were reading were simply a writer's personal approach, personal philosophy, or *"how I would do it."* In other words, these noble efforts to train without an emphasis on knowing and enforcing the rules of **THE GAME** were causing Officials to spend more time **learning to prevent** than learning to **enforce.** In other words, more Officials were being trained to be *"game managers"* than were being trained to be On-Court Game Officials. This type of training was, and still is, causing game Officials to make their on-court rulings based on *"something"* other than the rules.

If you have collected the ***NFHS Officials' Quarterly*** over the years, you'll find the below article on page 8 in the magazine published in the fall of 2004. I wish I still had as much hair as in the photo used in the article. I also wish I could testify to the amazing changes in officiating this article produced, but I have no way of measuring as to whether many or only a few Officials have found freedom by officiating as instructed by the Rules Book and the Officials Manual.

Remember, the below article was published in 2004 and was probably the beginning of my motivation to write this book. Free yourself from these misconceptions by becoming the Official **THE GAME** desires you to be. This will cause you to stop trying to decide **WHEN** to enforce the rules. If I were to write the same article today, the verb *call* would be changed to *rule* as that more accurately describes *"what we do"* as game Officials. We are constantly monitoring the activity and making **RULINGS.** Too often, Officials, Coaches, and Announcers think that the only time the Officials *"make a call"* is when we sound the whistle. Not true. In fact, a whistle is not needed in most of our *"rulings,"* since nearly everything the players do is legal.

Here is **"Prisoners of Damaging Misconceptions."**

"PRISONERS of Damaging Misconceptions" OFFICIALS' QUARTERLY/FALL 2004

According to Georgia Official Ray McClure, There Are Several Popular Words and Phrases That May Make High School Basketball Officials Prisoners of Damaging Misconceptions.

By Raymond McClure

These days, it seems that everyone has something derogatory to say about the way **THE GAME** of basketball is being officiated. Those of us who call **THE GAME** in ways we wish we did not may be prisoners of certain misconceptions about the rules and their enforcement.

The following is a partial list of some popular words and phrases . . . together with their twisted meanings . . . that may make high school basketball Officials prisoners of damaging misconceptions Feel for **THE GAME**: situational calling

Realistic officiating: ignoring certain rules

Controlling THE GAME: influencing the outcome of THE GAME

Call the obvious: ignoring violations and fouls that no one sees but you

Entertainment: THE GAME of basketball is not good enough entertainment in itself

Call selection: calls made depending on the score, the time, the player

Preventive officiating: allowing more than the three warnings allowed by rule

Let the players decide THE GAME: not enforcing the rules all the way until the end of THE GAME Sell the call: getting emotionally involved in THE GAME

Keep the foul counts even: cheating

Know the spirit and intent of the rules: knowing the tricks of the trade instead of the trade

Game management: doing something outside the rules

Advantage-disadvantage: not knowing the incidental contact rule

Most of us have used some of the above phrases at some time or another, maybe as recently as our last pregame conference. In fact, most of these phrases were created and adopted by the best basketball minds in the history of **THE GAME**. It's the way the phrases are misperceived that spells trouble for Officials. We cannot afford to allow these terms to take precedence over knowledge of the rules of **THE GAME** and proper mechanics.

With a thorough knowledge of the rules and proper mechanics, Officials can easily distinguish between a foul and incidental contact.

The following principles apply: Did the contact create an advantage for one player over another? Did the contact create a disadvantage of the other player?

If the Official has a patient whistle and sees the play from beginning to end, he or she will be able to make an accurate ruling by processing all of the needed information.

Violations, by contrast, must be called the same every game, every time, everywhere and by every Official. This can be accomplished if every Official will call violations by the rules, not trying to apply the advantage/disadvantage.

It seems as though many Officials use the following rationale for not calling some violations: He's barely out of bounds. She barely traveled. That was barely over and back. I remember calling three seconds once, but it was early in my career. Sure, he stepped inbounds before releasing the ball for the throw-in, but there was no defensive pressure.

Where does it stop? It never will, unless:

Officials stop applying advantage/disadvantage on violations. Officials start calling violations by the rules. Officials understand that incidental contact is only one of the many rules of **THE GAME**.

It seems that the phrase "call the obvious" has eroded to mean, "call only the obvious." We as Officials are taught to call the obvious.

Perhaps it should read, "Don't miss the obvious." However, near the end of **THE GAME**, with the team trying to stop the clock, Officials are told they don't have a "feel for **THE GAME**" if they really do call the obvious plays.

In that situation, how many times do you see obvious intentional fouls called common fouls? It's the same for touch fouls called late in **THE GAME** to help a team catch up. That really does show favoritism toward one team over another, since we do nothing to help the team that is ahead to maintain its lead.

Officials don't call **THE GAME** the same way, according to the rules. It doesn't matter what the score is, the time remaining or the number of personal or team fouls.

With a thorough knowledge of the rules and the application of approved mechanics, Officials can avoid being prisoners of all of these damaging misconceptions.

ABOUT THE AUTHOR: Ray McClure, who is from the metro Atlanta area, officiates in the American Basketball Association, the National Women's Basketball League, in NCAA Men's and Women's basketball, the NAIA, NJCAA, and high school. McClure founded the Five Star Referee Development Program, which includes a summer camp and a 12-hour classroom course, designed to teach the rules, mechanics and signals of officiating basketball.

OFFICIALS QUARTERLY, FALL 2004

And now, brethren, I reckon that through ignorance you did it, as did also your rulers.
—Acts 3:17

IF A THOUSAND
PEOPLE SAY
SOMETHING FOOLISH ABOUT THE TRUTH,
IT IS STILL FOOLISH.
TRUTH IS NEVER
DEPENDENT UPON
CONSENSUS OF BELIEF.

CHAPTER **10**

Officials Are Not Game Managers!

"Officiating Is Not a Management Session."

If a man stands with his right foot on a hot stove and his left foot in a freezer, some statisticians would try to convince us that, on average, he's comfortable. Obviously, nothing could be further from the truth. We are not to officiate with such an approach either. Having one foot on the Rules Book and the other on some game management approach to officiating has proven to produce game managers rather than Game Officials.

Over the years, there have been many *"opinions"* and descriptions as to what is the Role of a Basketball Game Official. Fortunately for **THE GAME**, none of our *"opinions"* matter, since our Role is clearly defined in our Support Books. Most opinions, I'm sure, have been expressed with good and noble intentions, while others were just cute and clever remarks. When younger Officials are in training, either at Summer Camps or in weekly training meetings, they perceive what they hear from the veteran Officials, as the *"gospel,"* because they assume that all veterans would be instructing them the same right way. They are impressionable, and they are eager to learn. However, too much of what is being taught has no rules support.

As is the case most of the time, these veteran Officials are simply quoting some slogan or cute remark they learned earlier in their careers. I know, as I was once guilty of the same. Let's all examine and then reexamine what we say as Basketball Officials, Trainers, and Supervisors, because unless our words have *"Book Support,"* what we say should always be suspect to being inaccurate, erroneous, ridiculous, and easily misunderstood.

I was told at my first summer camp, by a very high-profile retired Basketball Official, *"Now, Ray, either you have good judgment, or you don't. We can't help you with that."* I had no verbal response, but I recall the feeling I had upon hearing such from the Camp Director. I was already overwhelmed since I thought I knew the Rules before I got there. Now they can't help me *"judge accurately?"* It didn't make sense then, nor does it now.

> **If we Officials are to use *"judgment,"* then we will be *"judging."* If we are going to be *"judging,"* then the *"judging"* must be based on *"something."***

We often instruct Officials to think of themselves as the Courtroom Judge thinks of him/herself. They know the law. They have a court. They hear the evidence, and then they make a Ruling based on the gathered information. These Courtroom Judges are expected to make their Rulings based on the Law of the Land. Can you imagine a Courtroom Judge being referred to as the Courtroom Manager? It actually sounds demeaning, doesn't it? That's because it is. This Judge has spent many years studying the Law and has been elected by the people to **enforce** the Law, as written. I have seen tears running down the cheeks of a Courtroom Judge, as she sentenced the guilty party. She was the Judge and her ruling had to be accurate. Her promise to enforce and her commitment to uphold the Law would not allow her to rely on her *"feelings about the law."* She was the Judge and Judges must *"judge"* accurately.

The term *"Game Manager"* or *"Game Management"* is perceived by many as something Officials are **allowed** to do *"outside the rules."* Any time they are questioned about a ruling, their response has no rules support but is often characterized and justified, in their mind, as a *"managing moment."* Unfortunately, some games have dozens and dozens of such *"moments,"* and nearly every one of them are **"substitutes for rules enforcement."** Now multiply these *"managing moments"* times two or three Officials, and it becomes very clear why fans, players, and Coaches have no idea what the accurate ruling should be on block/charge, continuous motion, other contact, etc.

The only constant that Officials have at their disposal to ensure we all *"judge"* the same way . . . the accurate way . . . is the Rules. If Game Management has to do with *"people skills,"* then call it as such, but we all know it is actually using *"tricks of the trade"* to officiate *"outside"* the rules of **THE GAME.** Talking players out of the lane, keeping the foul counts even, issuing warnings and more warnings, deciding which rules are important and when to enforce them while officiating, etc.

When all Officials know these rules and enforce them, *"surprise rulings"* fade away, and the illusive consistency of **accurate rulings** begins to meet the expectations of everyone involved in **THE GAME.**

> The best *"game management"* approach is to *"know and enforce the rules of THE GAME."*

Anything that happens in **THE GAME** is covered within the Rules, whether it is high school or college basketball. The

Rules have been modified and adjusted for more than 125 years and are now clearly written. The main Role of Basketball Officials is to enforce the Rules as written. To do any less in the name of *"game management"* should be unacceptable regardless of one's nobility.

I recognize that there are some Officials who are Rules Nerds and they only have the ability to score very well on a written exam. They mentally cannot process the information fast enough to officiate a fast-moving game. This is a *"mental thing"* that we aren't smart enough to explain, but we can certainly recognize it when we see it. In addition, many of these Officials do not possess very good *"people skills."* This is not to be interpreted that these individuals are *"not good people;"* that is certainly not the case. In many cases, it is simply a personality matter and social skills that need improving.

The nice thing about becoming a Basketball Official is that each of us can always find games to officiate, which are suitable and match up with our skill level. If after five years of training and officiating games your organization continues to demonstrate a lack of confidence in your ability to officiate at the varsity level, you should continue to study, officiate lots of games, and be working on improving your weaknesses. In the meantime, be determined to become the Top-Ranked Official at the level where you are assigned.

No Varsity Official wants to be in a high-profile Varsity game with an Official whose skill level is at the eighth-grade level. It is most difficult to *"trust your partner"* in situations like this. However, an equally undesired crew member should be the Official who is constantly *"talking to prevent,"* giving unauthorized *"warnings,"* coaching the players, losing his/her composure, and *"negotiating his case,"* as though he is a *"lawyer"* and not the Judge.

> **We are the judge . . . not the lawyers! We are the Officials . . . not THE GAME managers! Our role is to judge and do so accurately, not to negotiate or prevent.**

Back in the late 1980s and early 1990s, there was one Official whom I really admired more than any other, and I was in the *"initial learning stages"* of my career. He was constantly on television (yes, we had TV back then), and when I heard he was going to be a Clinician at a certain Camp, I knew I wanted to be there. It did not take me too long, however, to realize he was a *"manager"* instead of a real, professional Basketball Official. I recall him saying, with a clever boldness, *"If you aren't talking ten players out of the lane in a game, you are not a good Official."* That's a *"game manager."* Game Managers are very good at using **"substitutes for rules enforcement."**

> **That's the type of inaccurate *"training"* that must stop! It is wrong!**

If that is what a college Supervisor wants you to do, then do it, but only because they instruct you to do so. These Supervisors may want to stop such requirements now that every fan has a camera and Video Review is now in their games. This approach should be an absolute *"taboo"* for NFHS Sanctioned Basketball Games. Let's all be reminded that high school games are played for different reasons than college or pro games. So take pride in being an Official, instead of allowing some *"managing philosophy"* to interfere with the life lessons the student athletes are to learn by participating.

Some leaders of high school groups brag about the fact that all their Clinicians at their summer camps are DI Officials. We have a very strong opposite opinion regarding our Camp Clinicians. We want Clinicians who have recently been in high school gyms, who have been trained on the differences in high school games and college games, who have been trained on the mission of the NFHS, regarding schoolboys' and schoolgirls' extracurricular activities. Due to the expectations placed on college Officials by their Supervisors and conferences, these high-profile college Officials seem to have very little to offer high school basketball Officials, during summer camps, that can be supported by the rules and/or the manual.

Here are a few other *"cute remarks"* that easily identify *"managers"* of games:

- *"We teach you to referee in the gray area."*
- *"Let the players decide THE GAME."*
- *"Make sure the fifth foul is a good one."*
- *"Just be consistent."*
- *"If it is a block on this end, make sure it is a block on the other end."*
- *"Call the obvious."*
- *"Develop a good call selection."*
- *"You have to learn to manage THE GAME."*
- *"Become a good play-caller."*
- *"You must control THE GAME."*

- *"We don't call that in this conference."*
- *"Call what makes THE GAME better."*
- *"Use the lightest touch to manage THE GAME."*
- *"Preventative officiating is a must."*
- *"Talk the players out of fouls and violations."*

And the foolishness continues . . .

> It is time for Basketball Officials to become experts at the **RIGHT THINGS** instead of endeavoring to be an expert at the **WRONG THINGS, such as**

- **Coaching the Players**
- **Counseling the Coach**
- **Assisting the Scorer and Timer**
- **Knowing the Number of Fouls on Each Player**
- **Knowing Who Gets the Next AP Arrow**
- **Using Unapproved Signals**
- **Talking to Prevent a Foul or Violation**

If Basketball Officials and clinicians would spend as much time teaching and learning the Rules, as they do in teaching Officials to *"stay out of trouble out there,"* then *"trouble"* would not find us. Let's all get better at knowing and enforcing the Rules that pertain to the **Jump Stop, Block-Charge, Traveling,** and **Continuous Motion** than we are at knowing how many fouls number 25 has committed.

I really don't know what you have been convinced or think *"game management"* is, but I can assure you of what it is **NOT**, and I know the NFHS agrees with the following, because the Rules Book is very clear.

> So in this section, NFHS is an acronym for <u>N</u>OT <u>F</u>OR <u>H</u>IGH <u>S</u>CHOOLS.

GAME MANAGEMENT IS NOT

- a replacement for rules and rules enforcement
- letting the players play
- being sure the fifth foul is a good one
- talking to players to prevent illegal activity
- letting the *"players decide THE GAME"*
- failure to penalize when THE GAME is on the line
- maintaining a *"flow"* to THE GAME
- controlling THE GAME
- keeping the foul counts even
- rulings made on this end of the court based on contact that occurred on the other end of the court such as *"If it's a charge on one end, it should be a charge on the other end."*
- preventive officiating
- warnings rather than rules enforcement
- warnings to avoid penalizing
- knowing the number of fouls on individual players
- knowing the number of time-outs a team has remaining
- keeping the star player in THE GAME
- Officials having their own tolerance level for coach and player conduct

Teaching all Officials to get good at *"game management"* is a major culprit, as there are various styles of management, with multiple personalities involved.

The Rules are for all types of players and all personalities and are not designed for allowances once the skill level is above teaching them how to dribble. Teaching all Officials a form of *"game management"* is so much more difficult than teaching them to officiate by the Rules while having excellent people skills and being a good communicator.

> **The most difficult part of officiating today is Officials trying to determine when to enforce the rules. That is shameful!**

Those who subscribe to the Role of Officials as Game Managers should learn and teach pages 82 and 83 in the Rules Book. That's where the role of the one and only Game Manager is clearly described.

Again, don't lower your position to that of a *"game manager,"* because we are more than that, and we need to accept our true identity (chapter 1) as Game Officials. When we officiate **THE GAME** by its rules and do so with excellent people skills and terrific verbal and nonverbal communication skills, we will stand head and shoulders above the Officials who lose composure, coach the players, *"smooze"* the coach, and incorporate *"situational call selection"* (ethics) in the name of *"game management."*

We recognize that many Officials who use this ambiguous term would never admit that they mean to *"manage instead of enforce,"* but that always proves to be exactly what they are doing. This was not their idea; this is what they have been taught. It is what I was taught. Too many are very confused, as they are constantly asking themselves, ***"Do I manage, warn, or enforce?"***

> *"Sports Officials are to officiate THE GAME by the rules of that game and never intentionally choose to avoid penalizing those who break them."*

> *They are only comparing themselves*
> *with each other, and measuring them-*
> *selves by themselves. What foolishness.*
> *—II Corinthians 10:12*

TO TRY AND GET ALL
OUR OFFICIATING
KNOWLEDGE BY
ONLY GOING TO
TRICKS, MYTHS,
PHILOSOPHIES, OR A
"FEEL," WILL NEVER GET US THE
RIGHT EDUCATION.

CHAPTER *11*

Substitutes for Rules Enforcement

"Stop Passing along Such Foolishness."

I have always been a notetaker whether in church, at business functions, or even Basketball Officials' summer camps. It is hardly an exaggeration when I state that my pen scarcely stops writing when I am focused and truly listening, regardless of the meeting. This chapter is all about remarks that are perceived as *"good training tips,"* which I maintain are noble efforts to share *"something"* with the audience that will make them better Basketball Officials. However, in too many cases, more harm has been done than good with some of these so-called *training tips*. What you are about to read below are comments that were used in an effort to *"train"* me and other Basketball Officials; some of which are continuing to be *"passed on"* to the present generation of game Officials.

Some will obviously appear to only be cute remarks, while others are about as ridiculous as can be. Hopefully, you will easily see the *"foolishness"* for what it really is: **a Substitute for Rules Enforcement.**

Since college games and pro games are played for different reasons than high school games, we cannot and should not condone *"beckoning of these substitutes"* into the high school gymnasiums. A Former NBA Official who was banned a few years ago was recently quoted regarding an out-of-bounds play, when he stated in an interview:

> *"Not only was it a jump ball, but based on the time and score in THE GAME, I would see most times giving the ball to the team that's behind in that situation. That's usually how the NBA referees do it."*

Well, if it's good for them, it must be okay for every other Official on the planet. Some would *"buy into"* this inadvertent cheating mentality and categorize it under *"game management."* Perhaps some Officials find comfort in the fact that **"You can't be bad or wrong, if there are no rules to follow."** Those who truly care for **THE GAME** should take the lead in removing this *"stuff"* or removing the Officials who continue to use such *"foolishness,"* instead of training Officials to learn and enforce the rules of **THE GAME.**

We must teach Officials that they don't need acronyms, principles, well-meant slogans, tips, or *"tricks of the trade"* if they will take the time to learn the rules. Most of today's listed principles and acronyms are a noble effort to assist Officials in their learning and enforcing the Rules that pertain to contact. When we dissect the rules, we find that all the principles and all the acronyms are thoroughly covered in the written word in the Rules Book. When leaders of officiating organizations actually learn the rules themselves, they will then be able to hold their staff accountable for all rulings, even contact rulings.

Okay, here is a list of actual quotes that I have *"heard with my own ears"* or read in *"training"* publications over the last three decades. Think about it, three decades of such *"nonsense training"* has resulted in today's Officials still arguing over the accuracy of Block/Charge, Continuous Motion, Traveling, etc. **Rocket Scientists are experts at their trade in less time.**

Here they are . . . word-for-word . . . no exaggerations. Read them slowly, and pretend you are sitting in the classroom hearing them for the first time while the *"trainer"* never references or uses a Rules Book. **I promise you that I have not embellished any of these.**

- o *"If you can't explain it . . . don't call it."*
- o *"If you don't know the rules . . . you'd better have good judgment."*
- o *"Get good at play calling."*
- o *"We teach you to referee in the gray area."*
- o *"Let the players decide **THE GAME**."*
- o *"Make sure the fifth foul is a good one."*
- o *"Be consistent; if it is a block on this end . . . make sure it is a block on the other end."*
- o *"You must have a feel for **THE GAME**."*
- o *"Learn to stay out of trouble out there."*
- o *"Let **THE GAME** come to you."*
- o *"Go with your gut."*
- o *"Referee strong!"*
- o *"Call the obvious."*
- o *"Develop a good call selection."*
- o *"Just be consistent."*
- o *"You have to learn to manage **THE GAME**."*
- o *"You must control **THE GAME**."*
- o *"We don't call that in this conference."*
- o *"You must recognize the spirit and intent of the rules."*
- o *"Don't call a technical foul unless it can improve **THE GAME**."*
- o *"Call what makes **THE GAME** better."*
- o *"Use the lightest touch to manage **THE GAME**."*
- o *"We have to take back control of **THE GAME**."*
- o *"Have the courage to enforce the rules."*
- o *"Learn to be an artist."*
- o *"When the players take **THE GAME** to another level, you must do the same thing."*
- o *"Preventive officiating is a must."*
- o *"Talk the players out of fouls."*
- o *"Talk the players out of the lane."*

How's your reaction so far? Are you laughing? Some are quite humorous. Does such *"training"* disturb you? It probably does, if you really are a **Guardian of THE GAME.**

Hold on to your seat, because here are some word-for-word quotes from a 1991 Publication titled *"Making the Call."* Again . . . *"word-for-word."* No enhancing.

o *"You are hired to make calls that control **THE GAME**."*
o Editor states, *"You must expand your knowledge of the rules and philosophy."*
o *"A ragged game calls for a different style of officiating than a smooth one."*
o *"Your purpose is to establish a calm environment for **THE GAME**."*
o *"If after you warn a player of dangerous activity prohibited by the rules, and the player persists, eject him from **THE GAME**."*
o *"Have guts. If you don't have guts, you'll be eaten alive."*
o *"Always try to talk players out of fouls."*
o *"You have to rise to the occasion, to the level of competition. If you can't, get out of officiating."*
o *"Avoid cheap fouls."*
o *"Don't be over officious."*
o *"Games get out of control when Officials start lying back and letting a lot of things go."*
o *"You want to let 'em play, but talk to them. Make them understand the parameters of what **YOU** are going to allow and what **YOU** are not going to allow."* (Emphasis on **YOU** is mine.)
o *"Officials can keep things under control by selling himself and his calls."*
o *"You need to give the impression that you know what happened, whether you actually do or not."* (My favorite.)
o *"Take what they give you and get out of the way. If it gets out of sync, then you take over."*

When we have Officials more concerned with *"keeping the foul counts even"* or *"keeping the star player in **THE GAME**,"* than they are at accurate block/charge rulings, **THE GAME** suffers, and in many cases, the Officials affect the final score. We must stop the suffering and discontinue forwarding the same *"stuff"* and the same *"foolishness"* that keeps getting the same results: **Inaccurate Rulings.**

Einstein said,

> *"Insanity is doing the same thing over and over and expecting different results."*

So the real culprit that causes each generation of Basketball Officials to continue to use *"substitutes for rules enforcement"* is the forwarding of nonrule-based *"garbage,"* non-Rules Book *"stuff"* that is a substitute for learning and enforcing the Rules of **THE GAME.** What other sport would condone such comments and characterize them as training? Volleyball? Golf? Tennis? Baseball? Football? All sports have Rules and the Rules are **THE GAME.** As I have stated so many times already in this book, ***"Why are we still discussing the accuracy of block/charge, continuous motion, traveling, etc. after 126 years."*** The answer is, ***"Officials are constantly trying to decide WHEN to enforce, WHEN to warn, and WHEN to officiate."***

I really believe I attended more officiating summer camps than anyone in history after reaching the *"old age"* of forty.

And in these camps, I have no recollection of a Clinician opening a Rules Book and showing me *"what I did wrong or right."* Never! What I did hear is listed above, and I really hope you will realize that such *"training"* is doing more harm than good, causing more confusion than clarity, and causing more hesitation than accurate response.

I repeat . . .

> ***"The most difficult issue for today's Officials is trying to determine when to enforce certain rules."***

When you hear a clinician make the statement, *"I wouldn't have called that."* I recommend you say nothing. However, this Clinician should be able to open the Rules Book and show you why he/she made such a statement. In addition, you should be suspect of being *"sold on a philosophical approach"* to officiating. Be warned and always remember:

"What Officials do on the basketball court should never be philosophical." Officiating can never be about *"what I would do"* or *"what you would do."* *"What we should do"* is clearly written in our support materials, which are the Rules Book, the Case Book, and the Officials Manual.

> *Wise people use knowledge when they speak, but fools pour out foolishness.*
> *—Proverbs 15:2, NCV*

IF YOU THINK THE RULES HAVE GRAY
AREAS, YOU NEED A
BETTER EDUCATION ON THE RULES.

—Ray McClure

AN E-MAIL FROM PETER WEBB

For nearly twenty years now, I have been fortunate to experience an ongoing friendship with Peter. He has never grown tired of training me with constant officiating *"nuggets,"* often in the early mornings or late evenings, usually after he was disturbed by something he saw on television, heard, or read regarding Officials and/or officiating. He had obviously just experienced a *"scratch-your-head, double-blink, what's-wrong-with-this-picture moment"* right before he sent the e-mail below, pertaining to social media discussion groups.

By the way, he is constantly asking me, *"Who anointed these people with the power to do as they please? This game is not theirs to mess with."*

Here is one of hundreds of e-mails from Peter, as he was venting in the late evening on June 16, 2013:

*****

Hello Raymond . . .

I wonder when Officials will understand that when they commit to officiating games at the schoolboy and schoolgirl level, they are agreeing to accept being part of the education process? Probably when their leaders understand it and then share it with them. Yes, realizing that sports, music and art are part of the community and school's curriculum. Officials are major keys to seeing that the participating youth take away from **THE GAME**'s experiences, the lessons which the school hopes for:

Planning, practice, hard work, goals, cooperation, teamwork, listening, caring, representing themselves and their family, their community and their school in public . . . even out of town . . . adjusting, winning, losing, failing, accomplishing, diligence, recovery, enjoyment and much more. All this resulting in untold life lessons learned and realized.

The NFHS rules code is designed to bring about the above mentioned personal and organizational (team) results. Officials must understand this in order to **serve the cause.** This understanding of purpose, beyond knowing the rules, is the zeroed-in-frame-of-mind that a crew of Officials should have upon leaving the dressing room.

Would you fall off your chair if the topic (Responsibility in the Role of Being Part of the Education Process) appeared within a discussion group? Have they ever wondered, *"Why are schools sponsoring sports?"*

If the people within these discussion groups (Facebook, Linked-In, etc.) were quality Officials they would not need to be involved in such discussions. Don't they understand that nothing they write is *"official?"*

Amen,
Peter
6/16/13

NEVER TAKE
DIRECTION FOR YOUR PERSONAL
CHOICES FROM A CROWD.

CHAPTER 12

Signals Are the Language
of **THE GAME**

"Do You Need An Interpreter?"

Several years ago, I went to Worcester, Massachusetts, to present the **Five-Star Basketball Referee Course** and my friend Ron Parker, of IAABO Board 26, had to serve as my *"interpreter"* as those folks, unlike we Southerners, speak with an accent. It didn't take too long before they all understood Southern and I understood the New England brogue, where they *"boycott"* the letter *R*. The good news was, even though we all had our accents, we were all actually speaking the English language.

The Bible tells us a story in Genesis 11 about the people in the land called Shinar, who wanted to build a Tower to Heaven, but when God changed their languages, they could not communicate with each other, and their foolish plan failed. In fact, with so much confusion and so many different languages, it all seemed like a lot of *"babble."*

> Unless we are all speaking the same language, it is most difficult, if not impossible, for a group of individuals to accomplish anything worthwhile.

I had the privilege to officiate some scrimmage games in the 1996 Olympics in Atlanta, where I have lived most of my adult life. We learned that we could not even *"try out"* unless we spoke the English language. It is a good thing that *"Southern English"* was accepted, as well.

Much of the communication used by Basketball Officials is a nonverbal form of communicating. This communication is with the use of **signals**. As we always teach, Signals are the Language of **THE GAME.** Signals are how Officials are to communicate with Partners, the Scorer, the Timer, and everyone else involved in **THE GAME.** As is the case with verbal communicating, it becomes very difficult to understand each other when we are *"speaking different languages."*

Ask yourself some of these questions:

- Do I *"speak"* the same Signals Language as is required by the Rules?
- Do I Signal with an *"accent?"*
- Do I communicate professionally, or do I *"do my own thing?"*
- Do I get emotionally involved and demonstrative when signaling?
- Do I choose to *"sell"* my rulings by drawing attention to my style of signaling?
- Do I pride myself in the use of Approved Signals, or do I choose to use unapproved Signals?
- Do I inform the fouler as to what he/she did wrong that caused me to sound the whistle?
- Or . . . am I a *"Hit-and-Run"* Official? (Hit the whistle and run to report?)
- Do I feel the noble necessity to further explain what happened, causing me to use unapproved Signals?
- Do I feel we need more Approved Signals?
- Do I feel that signals and signaling should be up to the Official?

In other words, what nonverbal language are you *"speaking,"* and are you sure that everyone totally understands what you are *"saying"*? Do you care?

Back in the *"old days,"* it was very obvious that the Officials in the Pro Game felt and acted as though they were *"part of the show."* They would nearly do cartwheels to demonstrate the *"and one,"* and you may even see one of them kissing a cheerleader, as part of the show. The high-profile TV Officials also became victim to much of this unprofessionalism, as well. All these shenanigans went away; and the Pro Basketball Officials began using more composure, dignity, and professionalism like the NFL Football Officials, who always seem to simply share their information as it should be shared.

Nowhere in the Rules Book or the Officials Manual are Officials instructed to *"sell their rulings"* to the Coach or anyone else. Most of this mentality started when Ex-Coaches and Ex-Athletic Directors became Supervisors of Game Officials. I recall one such Supervisor making the statement, *"You need to make sure the coach believes you got it right, whether you did or not!"* Things have not been the same since, as coaches now expect to be *"catered to"* and *"convinced"* that the Official *"got it right."* If they don't believe the Official, they have the right to *"rant and rave,"* seemingly, with the Supervisor's approval.

Can you imagine a retired Basketball Official being hired to be the *"leader"* of a Coaches Association? No? Neither can I. However, it sure seems to *"make sense"* to someone that Coaches and ADs are qualified to lead Basketball Officials' Organizations.

> **They proved to us that they didn't know the rules when they were on the sidelines, and now some DI conferences are led by individuals who have never been a game Official.**

What is on their resume that gets them hired to supervise Game Officials? I just don't get it. Can you imagine a Fire Chief never first being a Fire Fighter? Or a Police Chief who has never been a Police Officer? What about a School Principal who has never taught in the classroom? Do you see where I'm going with this? I'm sure many of these non-Officials who are now Supervisors of Officials have learned much about **THE GAME**, but their coaching mentality never leaves them. They want to be *"sold"* on the Official's Ruling. They often inquire, *"How could you call that with only sixteen seconds remaining."*

These Supervisors are no doubt very good individuals who care and desire to perform their duties as they should. However, they simply never really learned the Rules of **THE GAME** and **THE GAME** suffers because of their lack of truly understanding the real Role of Basketball Officials. They constantly demonstrate that they apparently believe that Violations are to be *"called by the rules,"* while Contact is to be *"judged by something else."* Perhaps a *"call selection"* . . . a *"feel for* **THE GAME***"* . . . a philosophy . . . or *"Well . . . that's his judgment."*

The necessity for possessing a uniform set of signals and resolute about Officials utilizing them is evident to everyone connected to **THE GAME**. Although the approved signals have been in existence for a long time, universal acceptance and proper usage have not occurred due to a lack of accountability. Signals are used to communicate and should never be used to draw attention to the Official.

The purpose of signals/signaling is to indicate what has or is happening. No signal is needed to indicate something has not happened (such as the, now approved, *"not-closely-guarded"* signal, the two-point goal or the blocked shot *"gator-chop"* signal).

The signals illustrated on the NFHS Signals Chart are those which have been established to convey needed information to fellow Officials, Scorers, Timers, Players, Coaches, Spectators, Media, and everyone involved in **THE GAME**. The use of unauthorized signals frequently confuse, as their meaning is unknown. Repeatedly, an unauthorized signal becomes the issue when problems occur during a game, as when one Official uses an unauthorized signal and a partner does not. Now the Table Crew (our Partners) is left wondering *"what exactly did happen."*

The use of additional signals or those given in an exaggerated manner does not help anyone. This is no time for the Official to get creative and emotional. Officials are not required or asked by basketball to *"sell calls."* They are only required to be accurate in their rulings and use the well-defined performance procedures.

Signals should be given in a manner which is calm, unemotional, under control, unhurried, dignified, informative, meaningful, and professional.

An Official on Friday night gives an unapproved signal, indicating that the scored goal was only two points and not three. On Saturday, the on-court Crew officiates as they should by only signaling when the point value of the goal is more than two points. We teach the Referee to inform the Table Crew that all scored goals are two points unless an Official indicates that a successful three-pointer has been scored. *"Overcommunicating,"* regardless of the nobility, is not needed, desired, or necessary.

Several years ago, a good friend of mine from Cartersville, Georgia, called me, and here is that conversation:

RAY. Hello.

FRIEND. Ray the Ref . . . I'll never do it again!

RAY. Hey, Ronny, what happened?

FRIEND. You've told me for years to stop showing a 2-Point Signal, but I did it last night. I was in the Center position, stuck my arm out showing two fingers. The Trail Official didn't count the number of fingers I was showing, and he thought I had signaled a 3-Point attempt. The ball went in, and he signaled as if the goal were a successful Three-Pointer. There was defensive pressure, so I didn't see his signal. We discovered this error much later in **THE GAME**, and it was too late to change it. I will never do it again.

The lesson here and the *"takeaway"* from this chapter is for Officials to discontinue all noble efforts to *"further explain and sell"* their rulings. What would happen if they didn't? Certainly nothing that isn't covered in the Rules of **THE GAME**. The Rules Committees have done a terrific job in selecting and approving signals that communicate what has occurred in **THE GAME**. Signals for what has **not** occurred are **not** needed or welcomed by *"Basketball."*

> **You don't need to give it more than 100 percent when using our nonverbal communications. Stop trying to go farther than necessary when signaling. Just *"master"* the signals chart, and only use the approved signals.**

If there is a blocked shot and the Official doesn't sound the whistle, obviously, the Official is not ruling a foul, so the foolishness of the *"Gator Chop"* demonstration is not needed, is not helping, is not clarifying, and is certainly distracting and quite foolish and unprofessional. Fans of this great game have the *"right"* to see the same signals every game.

When they don't, confusion is created, questions arise, and we are *"putting water in our own boats."* Be professional! Join the team! Improve communication and understanding by only using pre-scribed, approved, and dignified signals that have served our great game well for over 125 years.

What if you were directing traffic? Would you take a chance at being creative with your signaling? If you did, insurance rates would certainly increase in your area due to the increase in the number of traffic accidents.

> *When you talk, you should always be*
> *kind and pleasant, so you will be able to*
> *answer everyone in the way you should.*
> *—Colossians 4:6*

COMPLEXITY IS
YOUR ENEMY. ANY
FOOL CAN MAKE
SOMETHING
COMPLICATED. IT IS HARD TO MAKE
SOMETHING SIMPLE.

—Branson

CHAPTER 13

Philosophers In The Gym

"Middle C Never Changes, Because It Is Not Philosophical; It's a Law of Music."

I have played the guitar since I was a young teenager and began singing in church at age seventeen. It's what we PKs tend to do with encouragement from our parents. By the way, PK is an acronym for *"Preacher's Kid."* Even though I never took any music lessons, I knew what middle C was and where to find it on the piano and on my guitar. The cool thing about middle C is the fact that it was middle C yesterday and it will be middle C tomorrow; it will still be middle C after hundreds of years from now. I may sing *"off-key,"* and your piano may be out-of-tune, but, my friend, middle C remains **middle C.**

THE GAME of basketball has a *"middle C,"* and we need to stop trying to change it. Some modifications of the rules need changing from time to time, but haven't we had enough changes in the Rules to accommodate those who *"sing off-key,"* meaning those who don't play by the rules and Officials who don't enforce them? Instead of wanting to *"change the middle C,"* perhaps we need to *"retune our instruments"* and enforce the rules we already have. We need Officials to honor **THE GAME** by learning and then enforcing its rules. We need Supervisors and Assignors who hold their Officials accountable when they haven't learned the rules or when they choose not to enforce them. And, as we stated in other chapters, making an inaccurate Block/Charge ruling is indeed *"Kicking Rule."*

Again, just as *"God doesn't change"* (Malachi 3:6), **THE GAME** doesn't want or need us changing it just for the sake of changing it. I am convinced that there would be fewer requests for changes if the Officials and Supervisors had to *"prove their knowledge"* and be held accountable for their rulings. Leave **THE GAME** alone and enforce the rules, whether we like the rule or not. Not enforcing a rule for any reason could be viewed as a *"character issue,"* and no Official wants to be known as a *"cheater."*

> *"Learn and enforce the rules. The players will adjust, and the fans and coaches will know what to expect each time the whistle sounds."*

Unless we really know the history of a rule and *"why it is as it is,"* changing it to accommodate a lack of enforcement appears to be no big deal to those who make such suggestions. The same applies to Mechanics and Signals. Over the past three decades, we have become acquainted with a variety of *"approaches," "guidelines,"* and *"versions"* by which Officials are being instructed to *"call THE GAME."* Some have even gone so far as (are you ready for this?) to create their own *"philosophy,"* thus mandating their own *"unique way"* to officiate **THE GAME.**

Here is the definition of the word *philosophy*:

* **Noun . . .** *"a belief, or system of beliefs, accepted as authoritative by some group or school"*
* **Noun . . .** *"any personal belief about how to live or how to deal with a situation"*

If you are like me, you probably were appalled when you first heard that any organization would *"anoint itself"* with the power to officiate basketball in their own unique and personal way. The first time I was introduced to this *"very interesting training word"* was when

I began officiating NCAA D-I Women's Games. My last four years of college basketball officiating was on the women's side after sixteen years on the Men's side. However, upon further *"investigation,"* we did not find a ***"Philosophy of Officiating"*** but rather a ***"Philosophy for Officiating Contact"***—such as

- one hand staying on,
- two hands staying on,
- touching a player who is facing the basket,
- arm bar and hand,
- *"hot stove"* touch, and
- others . . .

I have memories of Officials ruling a foul for a slight touch with two hands, where there was absolutely **no foul**, as the contact was incidental. Then the same Official ruling a collision as incidental, because B1 did not put two hands on A1. This example is not a *"stretch of the truth,"* because I witnessed too many Officials relying on their ability to recall unique approaches, acronyms, and philosophies for that conference or skill level. The fans see boys' games, girls' games, men's games, women's games, and professional games. **THE GAME** and its followers would be much better off if everyone just got to watch **basketball games**.

I recognize that some levels have a Shot Clock and a wider lane, but

> *"Please leave the basic rules of basketball alone, so that a traveling violation is the same, so that a player control foul is the same, so that sportsmanship is the same, etc. If it is a violation at the high school level, there's no reason it shouldn't be a violation at the college level."*

During my final college season, I vividly recall three incidents that are worthy to discuss in this chapter about **philosophy**. All three involved different high-profile Women's College Basketball Officials who were serving as the Referee for the crew of Officials.

The first incident occurred in Alabama at Troy State University, in a very exciting basketball game, where the home team won by two points. When **THE GAME** ended and we were in our dressing room, we really felt as though we had officiated an almost perfect game. The hugs and high fives were bouncing off the walls, and the fans were going home after a thrilling home team victory. Troy State always gave us a box lunch to take on the road, as they were always a gracious host. The drive home to the north side of Atlanta from Troy, Alabama, was always very tiring, as Alabama is Central Time, while Georgia is Eastern Time. Nearly every game, I would leave the gym around 11:20 p.m. ET, with over 225 miles to drive, after running up and down the basketball court for almost two hours.

I recall being very alert that night, as the excitement of the environment was still buzzing in my head, continuing to hear the Head Coach say those words we all want to hear, whether we will admit it or not, *"Great job tonight!"* This game was one I wanted to have on video, so after Troy State mailed it to me, I couldn't wait to sit down with my Root Beer and watch it. However, if **THE GAME** had allowed coaches to *"challenge our rulings"* and force us to view the monitor for accuracy on Block/Charge and Continuous Motion, it still bothers me today to inform you:

The wrong team won THE GAME!

Two Player Control Fouls by the home team were inaccurately ruled as Blocking Fouls by the visiting team. Both would be perfect examples of what a Player Control Foul looks like. *"We kicked the same rule twice!"* Officials who know these contact related rules as they should before they are assigned games will not need anything other than that knowledge to achieve consistent, accurate rulings, assuming they have good eyesight and use proper mechanics.

There was one obvious Continuous Motion ruling that also was ruled in favor of the home team. Basketball Officials must make accurate rulings, and to the properly trained Official, it is obvious when they don't. All three of these very inaccurate rulings were ruled by the high-profile TV Official, and the visiting team did not have enough time to recover from these very inaccurate rulings. Most nights, we may affect the final score, but when we affect the outcome of a close game, we have failed in our required responsibility. No one could convince me that this Official had received a solid foundation of Rules Knowledge, upon which every officiating career should be built. She could run, she passed the *"eye test"* as she looked the part, and she used the latest style in *"unapproved signals."* However . . .

> **"Substance must come before style, as accuracy is found in the substance."**

On another instance, which also happened to be in Alabama, I was very excited to officiate with a longtime friend and high-profile DI Official. We were at Jacksonville State University and my friend was the Referee, so he was leading the discussion in our Pregame Conference. When we got to the discussion on **contact**, he stated,

> **"I'm not going to discuss one hand staying on, touching with two hands or an arm bar and a hand being used at the same time. All three of us should know what contact is a foul and what is not."**

To which I replied, ***"Thank you . . . I agree a hundred per-cent."*** **WOW!** How refreshing! He was a top-ranked TV Basketball Official, who was held in high esteem throughout our officiating world, and his character and integrity were above reproach. Quality Officials will see the effect the contact has on the opponent and be able to quickly determine whether the contact is legal or illegal. I will state here that this was before the Rules Book contained the contact mandates of two hands on, touching the opponent more than once, etc. You see, once the Rules Book has such in print (NFHS 10.7.12) (NCAAW 10.1.4), it is no longer a philosophy but a rule. And game Officials have no choice but to enforce the *"written word."* This is an example of a rule change that was not needed. All that was needed was THE GAME Officials to master the rules pertaining to contact.

Let me insert here that an Official's personal judgment is only accurate judging when there is written rules to support the judging.

The third game that comes to mind when I think of the word *"philosophy"* was another game, believe it or not, that was also played in my neighboring state of Alabama. It was a beautiful Saturday in February, and we were in Birmingham at Samford University. The Referee in this game was also a very high-profile Official who was usually seen on television on Saturdays at major DI schools. However, on this day, she was leading the Pregame Conference for us at Samford. To her credit, she was very detailed, organized, and obviously took pride in her ability to go down the Pregame Checklist, as every good Referee should do.

When she got to the part about **contact**, she never mentioned anything about officiating by the rules, but instead *"struck a nerve with me"* when she moved into the philosophical *"Bull"* that I had heard for the last too many seasons. As I indicated, this was February, and I already knew I was retiring from college officiating at the end of the season, so I could not pass up the chance to say what I had wanted to say for a long time. Of course, I was polite and respectful, but I had to respond, and I'm still glad I did. **THE GAME** needs a *"voice"* to stand up for it. You and I can be that *"voice."*

This Official is a very nice person, and she appeared to officiate exactly as instructed by the NCAA Women's **philosophy**, as I had heard this often since switching to the Women's game four years prior. However, when she made the statement that is so far from rules enforcement, I knew I had to ask a question. She said, *"If it's a block on this end . . . let's make sure it's a block on the other end."* I then respectfully asked,

> *"You want us to make a call on the other end, based on the contact that occurs on this end?"*

She replied, *"No, Ray, you know what I mean,"* which caused me to say, *"No, I don't."*

She offered no further remarks, and I'm sure she was thinking, *"This guy just doesn't get it."* Well, that was totally accurate. I don't get it. Why not learn and then enforce the rules as written and get rid of these concerns about what others think? Make accuracy the goal, instead of *"pleasing others."* If I recall correctly, her next topic in the Pregame Conference was something about *"keeping the foul counts even."*

I remind us again of the Referee's attitude at Jax State, which he was basically stating that *"Surely, each of us knows what a foul is."* To which I submit . . . and these are my words:

> *"If you don't know what a foul is by now, what are you doing at the DI level, and who hired you?"*

The main role of Basketball Officials, beginning around the Sixth-Grade Skill Level of play, is **consistent, accurate rulings**. That cannot be accomplished with an individual or organization's *"philosophical approach"* to officiating. Perhaps this type of officiating is perfect before the sixth-grade age group, because the coaches and the Officials know that this is the age where the players are to be learning the skills necessary to enjoy **THE GAME** and have fun in doing so. By the sixth grade, the players should be able to catch the ball, dribble, pass, shoot, and play by the rules.

Those who use a **philosophical approach** to officiating would never admit or even think they are doing something that is outside the rules of **THE GAME**. Their efforts are noble, and they are very good people. However, the leaders and Supervisors need to be reminded that **consistent, accurate rulings** can never be accomplished by an individual, nor a group, until each of us becomes committed to **THE GAME**, with no concern as to what coaches or anyone else thinks about our rulings. With all the video cameras and instant replay capabilities, one must wonder how any Official can justify any approach other than an enforcement of the rules.

As **PETER WEBB** has ingrained in me for years, we all need to understand that

> *"Every ruling we make matters to both teams; and sports-manship, courtesy, and rules enforcement are not enemies of fair play and competition."*

Philosophies do not *"hold water"* in a negligence lawsuit. The Judge only wants to know **"What do the rules instruct you to do?"** If protests were allowed, philosophies would be irrelevant. The State Associations must answer to the schools, and the Principals don't want to hear your personal philosophy; they want to see a Rules Book because that's where the **accurate decision** is to be found.

No philosophy for officiating **violations** was found in print anywhere. That certainly is good news, since everyone involved in **THE GAME** should know that *"advantage/disadvantage"* is never to be considered when making a **violation** ruling. It appears that those organizations who admit to using a philosophical approach are instructing their Officials to officiate **violations** by the rules and officiate **contact** by *"something else."* I am convinced that this approach is not necessary, because . . .

> **The rules pertaining to contact are just as clearly written as those regarding violations.**

However, since too many feel that *"judgment is a personal thing,"* too few Officials even bother to learn Rules 10.7, 4.23, 4.24, 4.27 and 4.11. (NFHS). If there needs to be basic reminders to assist Officials in the enforcement of the rules of **THE GAME**, that is certainly not the issue. However, the word *philosophy* will always be a dangerous word to use when training Basketball Officials, as a philosophical approach leads to a lack of **consistent, accurate rulings.**

There is an obvious distinction between those who officiate by the Rules and those who use an organization's or personal philosophical approach. First, we hear these Officials make comments like, **"Call the obvious,"** and then fail to penalize players who obviously step into the lane too soon, hang on the ring and don't resume play on the second horn following a time-out. We hear *"philosophical Officials"* say, **"We don't call that in this conference."**

I recall a game I was officiating at Florida A&M University in Tallahassee my first year in the MEAC. I was the Official with the ball during a time-out. So when the second horn sounded to **end** the time-out, I ended it as we were instructed by the Resumption of Play Procedure at that time. I followed the exact instructions, which I had learned from the Rules Book and the CCA Manual:

1. **I sounded the whistle,**
2. **gave the directional signal,**
3. **placed the ball on the floor at the disposal of FAMU,**
4. **then . . . began the five-second throw-in count.**

When the players realized that I was enforcing the rules, they hustled to get the ball and completed their throw-in without a violation.

At halftime, the Referee in this assignment told me, *"Ray, we don't do that in this conference."* I asked, *"Do what?"* To which he responded, *"Put the ball down after a time-out."* I then asked, *"Are there other rules I need to know about that we are not allowed to enforce in this conference?"* His reply was simply, *"We don't do that."*

What was interesting was, and I promise this is true, in the second half, the exact same situation occurred, where I was the Lead Official with the ball; and when the first horn sounded, the players ran out of the team huddle, leaving the coach talking, to come to me for the throw-in. I recall thinking,

> *"Wonder why anyone would not enforce a rule that is so easy to enforce accurately?"*

We need to accept the fact that a philosophical approach is filled with inconsistencies, tolerances, and preventive officiating. Some will argue that we Officials should prevent as many violations and fouls as possible, while others immediately wonder, *"Where did that mentality begin?"*

The word *philosophy* strongly implies that the Official can use his/her own tolerance level when serving as a game Official. Never forget this truth, and it is a direct quote from **PETER WEBB:**

> *"Tolerance always favors one team over the other!"*

Too many Officials fail to remind themselves that there are always two teams involved and always two teams to consider. Everything we Officials do affects both teams. Our role is to be accurate in everything we do, and our accuracies are determined by *"What thus sayeth the word."* (Like I said, my father was a minister.)

Think about this: We allow A2 to play illegally by removing the whistle from our mouth and instructing A2 to *"Get out of the lane!"* B2 is then waiting and wondering what good assistance we are about to share with him/her to avoid a violation on their part. The Rules only allow for four warnings, yet we hear Officials issuing warnings constantly and consider it preventive officiating. I am convinced that this is a noble effort to make the contest better, and this *"Substitute for Rules Enforcement"* continues to be passed from one generation to another, regardless of how wrong it is. And . . . **IT IS WRONG!** By the way, the 2017 NFHS rules changes included Official warnings to the Head Coach. These two rule changes have nothing to do with the referenced four above.

> *Once basketball Officials are thoroughly trained in their actual role as a game Official, they will no longer care if a player commits a violation or care if a player commits a foul.*

The coach should care. Not us. It is not our role to care. Efforts to prevent is an obvious *"caring,"* and soon people will begin to wonder *"if we care who wins."*

The main purpose of this chapter is to *"seek to find the right words"* that will cause each of us to rethink any *"approach to officiating"* that contains these ubiquitous *"Substitutes for Rules Enforcement."* The difficult part here is to convince veteran

Officials that a philosophical approach is always filled with *"substitutes for Rules Enforcement."*

> **Nowhere can we find support for anything that is philosophical. Our role is clearly defined, and it doesn't allow for me to officiate differently than you do.**

Obviously, we have different personalities and different people skills, but each of us should be Rules Experts who *"monitor the activity"* and make **Accurate Rulings** based on that activity. This is our Role, and we are to *"go about our assigned tasks"* with no regard to *"**Who** has the ball, what the **score** is nor the **time** remaining in* **THE GAME.**"

Again . . . when we really analyze a Philosophy, it will always contain an *"approach"* that is opposite to what basketball asks us to do and the Head Coaches will be asking, *"What is your personal philosophy? How will this crew be 'calling'* **THE GAME?**"

- **Philosophies are a *"personal thing,"* which means we are allowed to do things our way.**
- **Philosophies are permission to choose when or when not to enforce the Rules.**
- **Philosophies are excuses to talk instead of enforce.**
- **Philosophies allow Officials to *"look the other way"* in the name of a *"feel for THE GAME."***
- **Philosophies permit the Official to have a personal *"call selection."***

Don't be afraid to be known as a Rules Expert. That is the exact requirement we should have before we get on the court to officiate our first Varsity game. Does that mean we know everything? Certainly not. However, we should want to. Rules Enforcement is a much better and safer *"approach"* than trying to be a philosopher. Popular style, popular philosophy, and popular *"tricks of the trade"* can never have **THE GAME**'s best interest in mind. **THE GAME**, when played by the rules, is great entertainment. **THE GAME** is bigger than any one person; is bigger than any one organization; and deserves our honor, dignity, and pride. And it deserves to be preserved.

> **The rules are a matter-of-fact; ideas, philosophies, and personal approaches are a matter of personal opinion.**

The way of a fool seems right to him,
but a wise man listens to advice.
—Proverbs 12:15

IT IS USELESS TO
ATTEMPT TO REASON
A MAN OUT
OF A THING HE
WAS NEVER
REASONED INTO.

CHAPTER **14**

"No Calls" Are a Myth

"Officials Make Rulings . . . Not Calls" (Peter Webb).

There is always a *"call,"* even when there is no whistle sounded. There is **never** a *"no-call."* When there is no whistle, the *"call"* was a **Ruling** of legal activity. Did you get that? Do you need to read that again? Just in case . . .

> *"There is no such thing as a 'no call.'"*

Thinking in terms of **Rulings** vs. *"calls"* is really a much more accurate and professional description of what we do as Game Officials. Thinking in this manner will cause us to rid ourselves of the inaccurate and uninformed language that is used by the *"talking heads"* on television and others who are not part of this *"family of Game Officials."* As is covered in another chapter, the *"real role"* of a Game Official is to *"monitor all activity and then make **Rulings"*** that are based on what we see and hear. Those **Rulings** are either Accurate or Inaccurate, based on the Rules of **THE GAME**. Nothing else.

More than thirty years ago at an upstate New York University, a very interesting experiment was performed on a Basketball Official. The *"Study"* was designed to have a better understanding of the many thoughts and decisions made by an on-court basketball Game

Official during an actual basketball game. The wiring apparatus was designed to measure Brain Waves, caused by thoughts, which were triggered by images seen and sounds heard. It was discovered that Basketball Officials process a tremendous amount of information and do it at, seemingly, *"the speed of light."*

The results of this very interesting *"Study"* showed that the Basketball Official made more than 1.4 million *"calls"* during that game. Obviously, we Officials are constantly processing information to make **Accurate Rulings**. Since there are *"not quite one million whistle sounds"* heard during a game, the clear *"takeaway"* from the *"Study"* is the fact that players play legally much more than they play illegally. Therefore, Officials make more Rulings on legal activity than they do on illegal activity. Once again, proving that *"No-Calls"* are a myth. Therefore, we never *"pass on it."*

We always make a ruling, and sometimes the sound of a whistle is heard.

Another needed clarification is the fact that no **Rulings** can *"go either way,"* as all **Rulings** are either accurate by rule or inaccurate by rule. If the **Ruling** is inaccurate, no amount of selling will cause it to be accurate. Our Role is to make **Accurate Rulings**. Period. The only way to know if they are accurate is to compare them with *"what thus sayeth the word,"* which is the Rules Book.

When we Officials think in this manner, we will begin realizing that there is also no such thing as a *"Ticky-Tack-Foul,"* since the Rules Book is clear as to what contact is legal and what contact is illegal, what contact is Incidental, and what contact is a Foul (see the chapter on *"Ticky-Tack"* Fouls).

We have all heard the Coach or a fan yell, *"Come on, Ref, let 'em play."* That is exactly what we are charged with doing. We are to *"let 'em play."* However, we are required by Rule to *"Let **both** teams play."* And . . . their *"playing"* must be by the Rules. I recall a Coach who once yelled to our Crew, *"Come on, Ref . . . let 'em play."* I could tell that my response caused him to really think or rethink his comment. All I said was,

> *"I was trying to let them play, Coach,*
> *but your guy fouled him."*

Again, our role is to *"let both teams play."*

We are the *"Judge"* in our *"courtroom,"* which is normally 84' X 50' or 94' X 50'. We are using *"judgment"* as we *"monitor all activity."* This *"judgment"* is our **Rulings**. And like a Judge in a legal courtroom, these **Rulings** must be based on the *"Law of the Land."* For us, it is the *"Law of the Court;"* the basketball court. Do not allow yourself to have an unhealthy fear of the Rules of **THE GAME**. We are to honor **THE GAME** by enforcing its Rules.

The judge in a courtroom doesn't make *"calls."* He/she makes **Rulings**, and those **Rulings** are to be based on the law. The judge is to use judgment that can be supported by the law. Judgment that is based on anything else usually causes the judge to lose his/her next election.

In our *"court,"* we are to judge the activity and then make **Rulings**, then penalize illegal activity, based on our law, which is well defined in the Rules Book. When we Officials judge inaccurately, the *"law of THE GAME"* is not being enforced as it should be. We are paid to **rule with accuracy**. Officials who judge inaccurately cannot be excused by their supervisor saying, *"Well . . . that's his judgment."* If *"his judgment"* doesn't have rules support, then ***"he is judging inaccurately."*** There is no room for consistent, inaccurate rulings.

> **Accurate rulings can only be determined by comparing the judge's judging with the law, and our *"law"* is the RULES OF THE GAME.**

A double-minded man is unsta-
ble in all his ways.
—James 1:8

DEFENDING YOUR
FAULTS AND ERRORS
ONLY PROVES THAT
YOU HAVE NO INTENTIONS OF
QUITTING THEM.

CHAPTER 15

Basketball Officials Can't Have Their Own "Strike Zone"

"The Tricks of the Trade versus the Trade"

I am a huge baseball fan and have been since the mid-1950s when Davy Crockett was so popular that my new baseball had his name and image on it. Go figure. Baseball and Davy Crockett? Now that's marketing.

Major League Baseball has always demonstrated much pride in maintaining the *"purity and integrity of baseball"* and never tolerated any exceptions, regardless of how popular and well-known some star player may be. From the 1919, White Sox, who became known as the *"Black Sox"* for decisions by a few to intentionally lose the World Series, to Pete Rose's gambling charges and the steroid era, MLB has never wavered on its integrity commitment toward its game.

I share this because I attended a Baseball Umpires' Camp shortly after I became a Basketball Official. I was about forty-two years old and not as impressionable as those half my age who were also in attendance. However, some of what I was taught did not match up with the *"Integrity of Baseball,"* and it disturbed me. Witnessing experienced Baseball Umpires *"admitting"* to having their own Strike

Zone—and even changing it during **THE GAME**—depending upon the count, the score, and the batter was bothersome.

To illustrate his point regarding a 3–0 count, one Umpire told us, *"If the next pitch is anywhere between the two dugouts, I call it a strike."* Obviously, an exaggeration, but the message he was sharing was very far from enforcing the Rules of Baseball.

> **When sports Officials waver and intentionally fail to enforce a rule, these Officials need to recognize that their so-called *"feel for THE GAME"* is a serious intentional failure to perform the required duties of a judicious game Official. THE GAME has rules and Officials are to enforce them.**

In fairness to them, if anyone accused them of being a *"cheater,"* it would really hurt them as they truly believe that honesty, integrity, and character are at the core of Sports Officials. They, like many of us, have been taught that certain *"tricks of the trade"* are useful and necessary to be a *"good umpire."* These *"tricks"* are substitutes for rules enforcement, regardless if they are referred to as *"game management,"* *"call selection,"* or *"feel for THE GAME."*

Softball is a *"version"* of Baseball, and regardless of one's skill level, teams are always looking for players. Even today, I continue to enjoy the sport as a Senior Softball Player and play in a local league here in Woodstock, Georgia. In addition, National Senior Softball Organizations have monthly tournaments for traveling teams that are made up of those who are skilled enough to be selected to play in their age group. Those of us who play the infield often have bruises that cause us to wonder why our game is called **soft** ball. Trust me, if it were soft, these sixty-five-year-old men would not still be hitting it 375 feet.

Even after all these years of baseball and softball, occasionally, a player will make a comment expressing his *"fear"* of us getting on the umpire's *"bad side,"* meaning if the ump is upset with us, he will make calls that favor the other team. Every time I hear such, I feel obligated to remind them, ***"We should not be concerned about such if the umpire has integrity."*** Yes, I make sure the umpire hears me when I say it. Unfortunately, this is a legitimate concern because too many Sports Officials think they can do as they please and make **THE GAME** about themselves.

If you read the acknowledgements of this book, you'll notice that one of the two individuals to whom I dedicated this book is **PETER WEBB**. Peter has been a dear friend and mentor to me and has proven to be a true Guardian of **THE GAME**. When I first introduced Peter to Joe Conley, another dear friend and former Minor League Baseball Umpire, Peter's first words as he shook Joe's hand were, ***"Do you have your own strike zone?"*** The question took Joe by surprise, and as the years have passed, Joe and I have become much better Basketball Officials because of that introduction and the many other lessons learned from Peter. There is a Strike Zone in Baseball and Umpires can't make accurate strike rulings unless they know what that Strike Zone is and are skilled enough to recognize exactly where the pitched ball is regarding that Strike Zone. If they call a pitch a *"ball"* when, by rule, it is a *"strike,"* that umpire has *"kicked a rule of baseball."* This is accepted by the masses if the umpire is consistent. Well, being consistently inaccurate, being consistently wrong, or having your own strike zone does not honor **THE GAME**.

A few years ago, the company that created the technology that shows the television audience where the pitch was located asked a Major League Umpire, ***"Why did you call that pitch a strike that was eleven inches off the plate?"*** The well-known high-profile Major League Umpire's response still concerns me today, as he said, ***"THE GAME needed a strike."*** I hope you also find that disturbing. It is this kind of *"stuff"* (remember, we are calling it *"stuff"*) that is one of the motivations behind the writing of this book.

Basketball Officials can learn lessons from our Baseball Umpire Friends; one of which is **we cannot have our own interpretation of what a *"strike"*** (foul or violation) **is.** We are to enforce the rules as written, and the rules pertaining to violations and contact are clearly written.

I continue to be amazed at the number of Basketball Officials who have learned the *"Tricks of the Trade"* and have never taken the time to become an expert at the *"Trade."*

> **THE GAME deserves better, and those of us who really care about THE GAME and the actual role of game Officials would love to see someone, some leader, all leaders come forward and hold all Officials accountable for any substitute for rules enforcement.**

Are you aware of the number of Summer Camps that an Official attends in his/her first ten years of officiating? Perhaps you are an Official who desires or desired to officiate at the college level, and you spent the money to attend three or four or five Summer Camps to be seen and then hired by a Supervisor and placed on a college conference Officials' staff. If so, think back to what was taught. Did you receive presentations on Traveling, Guarding, Verticality, Continuous Motion, etc.? In nearly all cases, the answer is, *"No. I did not receive such presentations."*

Obviously, there are exceptions because these topics are taught in detail at our Five-Star Referee Course and our Camps and the IAABO Camps (Schools). However, for the most part, Summer Camps teach **mechanics** and some philosophical approach to officiating. In addition, we hear Clinicians say things like, *"I wouldn't have called that."*

"Why would you make that call at a time like this?" "Are you aware of the time on the clock?" "Were you not aware that number 23 already had three fouls?" "How did you all let the foul count get so lopsided?"

I walked up behind one of my Clinicians, who was serving at one of our **Five-Star Officials Camps**, and he was talking to the Crew at halftime of a game. Even though he did not know I was listening, I was not sneaking up on him. He just said the wrong thing at the wrong time. Anytime would be the *"wrong time"* to say what he said. Regardless, I was very disappointed when I heard him make this statement, which I'm sure he thought was *"good training,"* since he had learned it in college camps. He told these Officials, *"If a player looks down and sees he has both feet on the three-point line and then steps back with one foot and then the other so he now has both feet behind the line, I can live with that."*

This is clearly a Traveling Violation that the Clinician is teaching Officials to ignore and thus condone. Since he is teaching this, one can't help but ask a few investigative questions:

- *"Who taught him that it is okay to live with such?"*
- *"What other violations can he personally live with?"*
- *"How many other Clinicians across the country are teaching the same nonsense?"*
- *"Where do these people get approval or who anoints these people with permission to officiate outside the Rules?"*

We even hold these same Officials up as our models and put their pictures on covers of magazines while they are showing an unapproved signal, then reading published articles that are filled with this same *"stuff."* **THE GAME** is what we should be holding up as the model—not Officials who refuse to comply, not Officials who have become experts at the things they are **not** asked to do by basketball while failing at the true assigned task of a *"real"* Basketball Official.

> **When we leave Officials unchecked and unaccountable, they mimic one another, and the overall performance of Officials does not measure up to the expectations of *"basketball."***

These *"Tricks of the Trade"* have produced Officials who have *"feet that are better educated than their heads."* In other words, we have gotten really good at the Mechanics but not at the Rules. We have gotten really good at the *"tricks"* but not at the *"trade."* Why stand in the right spot to get the best look if you don't know what you are looking for? We constantly see perfectly positioned Officials who make inaccurate block/charge rulings, inaccurate continuous motion rulings, and rule the *"spin move"* as legal foot movement even though the player in control of the ball lifts the pivot foot and places it back to the floor while still holding the ball.

Training Basketball Officials is very serious business and should not to be done by individuals who are not Rules Experts. Clinicians will teach what they know. If they only know *"tricks"* that is what they teach. If they are Mechanics experts, teaching Mechanics will come easy. My point is . . .

> **The rules are to be mastered first . . . not mechanics, not signals.**
> *"We can't make accurate rulings, if we don't know the rules."*

How do you truly feel about this topic? Do you think there is an acceptable time to *"look the other way"* instead of enforcing the rules? If you do, it is because someone has taught you that it is okay—perhaps someone whom you hold in high esteem. Perhaps you also heard this same person make one or all of these statements:

- *"I've officiated for years, and I've never really been a rules guy."*
- *"He doesn't know the rules, but he has good judgment."*
- *"He wasn't a rules guy, but he was a great Official."*

Can you imagine hearing doctors, lawyers, pharmacists, or teachers making statements like this about their profession? What if your child were going into surgery and you overheard the surgeon admitting that he gets by, gets through it, but he really wasn't an expert in his field? The truth is, these professionals are indeed experts because they are required to be. They are required to prove it. Are they perfect? Probably not. However, they are held to a very high standard and **THE GAME** of basketball expects us to take the same approach, and **WE ARE NOT DOING THAT!**

Just because we stayed at a Holiday Inn Express last night doesn't make us a qualified Basketball Official. We are only qualified after we have learned the **RULES**, know the proper **MECHANICS** system, and use approved **SIGNALS**. These three are the foundation, and the foundation must be built first. Then, and only then, can we learn **HOW** to officiate. We must stop promoting Officials until they have the proper foundation upon which to build an officiating career.

To repeat . . . that foundation is a **thorough knowledge of the Rules, knowledge of the Proper Mechanics, knowledge of the Approved Signals,** *"Why Schools Have Sports,"* and the *"Importance of Rules and Rules Enforcement."*

***

Too many Officials want to be discovered . . . not developed.

***

> *Therefore, to the one who knows*
> *the right thing to do and does*
> *not do it, to him it is a sin.*
> *—James 4:17*

**TIME TO STOP DEBATING AND
START KNOWING.**

CHAPTER 16

Contact Is Also Rules-Based

"Contact Rulings Are Not About Your Personal Feelings"

To make the statement *"There is Contact in THE GAME of basketball"* is about as eye-opening as informing someone that fish get wet when they swim. One may think that Rule 4, where definitions are listed alphabetically, would have **contact** listed between Closely Guarded and Continuous Motion; but it is not defined there. However, the Rules Book (all levels of play) is very clear that **Contact** does occur and clearly defines the two types of contact as **Legal** and **Illegal**.

Illegal Contact is defined as a **Foul**, while **Legal Contact** is defined as **Incidental** (NFHS 4.27); it is *"just contact"* that occurs due to there being ten players moving around in a confined space.

The purpose here is to increase awareness that Officials can and should be seeking **Consistent, Accurate Contact Rulings**, instead of *"anything else,"* and to establish the fact that Officials can only know the difference between these two types of well-defined contact, if they **Know the Rules** that apply to both types. *"You can't make accurate rulings on rules you don't know."*

Have you ever heard someone say, *"He doesn't know the rules, but he has good judgment?"* The truth is . . .

> **It is impossible to have accurate judgment without knowing how to judge, since judging must be based on *"something"* and that *"something"* is the rules of THE GAME.**

Doesn't everyone have the right to expect Officials to officiate by the rules? Of course they do. This is a reasonable expectation, because when Officials don't officiate **THE GAME** by its Rules, regardless of the reason, **Inaccurate Rulings** are the end result.

We recently heard of a crew of Officials who were penalized for misapplying a Team Control Rule during a throw-in.

The bottom line is they *"kicked a rule."* But the good news is they only *"kicked it"* once. However, it seems that Officials are never penalized or reprimanded for **Inaccurate Contact Rulings**, such as **Inaccurate Block-Charge Rulings**, **Inaccurate Continuous Motion Rulings**, etc. Rulings on these **Contact** situations occur many times a game. These **Inaccurate Rulings** are the same as *"kicking a rule."* If we knew we were going to be penalized or reprimanded, would we find a way to stop *"kicking these rules"*? Of course, we would.

Too often we hear the leaders say, *"Well . . . that's his judgment,"* as if to imply that this Official never makes an inaccurate ruling; he just has *"different judgment"* than other Officials. However, when the same Official misses an out-of-bounds ruling, observers say things like, *"He sure kicked that one." "She was looking right at it. How could she miss that?" "What was she thinking?" "Why didn't she ask for help?"*

But regarding **Contact Rulings**, we again hear, *"Well . . . that's her personal judgment,"* and the Official moves on to the next round in the tournament taking that *"poor and inaccurate judging"* with her/him—many times affecting the outcome of **THE GAMES** she/he officiates.

THE GAME of basketball is more than 126 years old, and during this time, we Officials have mastered many rules while failing to do so with others. For example, see how you do on this True or False Quiz:

- **When the ball goes in the basket from above points are scored. True or False?**

- **An out-of-bounds violation occurs when a player steps on a boundary line while holding or dribbling the ball. True or False?**
- **The free thrower can attempt free throws without being guarded. True or False?**

How did you do? My guess is, you knew the correct response to be **True** for all three of these. These are rules we have mastered. Our **Judgment** was very good on these three. But why were we able to **Judge Accurately**? Certainly not because of someone's personal approach or their **Unique Judgment**. Instead, because we have learned these rules. We have rules support! We can provide proof!

> It is time for each of us to accept the fact that the *"judgment of Officials"* is only accurate judging if it can be supported by the rules of THE GAME.

It may serve us well to know that there are only sixty-eight small pages that contain the ten Rules of **THE GAME**, and they are very clearly written. So if they are clearly written, then Officials should be able to clearly understand them. It is becoming more evident that Officials and their leaders continue to approach **THE GAME**, as if violations are to be *"Judged by the Rules,"* but **Contact** is to be judged by *"Something Else."* However, if all the rules are clearly written, and Officials can learn to make accurate rulings that pertain to **Violations**, they can also learn to make accurate rulings that pertain to **Contact**.

Contact should be ruled a foul because the **Rules** say so and for no other reason. It is time for all of us to realize that the **Rules** pertaining to **Contact** are just as clearly written as those for violations. The *"written word"* in Rule 10.7 (NFHS) is quite impressive, as it clearly informs the reader of what players are allowed to do and prohibited from doing. Again . . . clearly written . . .

- **What the PLAYER can and cannot do . . .**
- **What the DRIBBLER can and cannot do . . .**
- **What the SHOOTER can and cannot do . . .**

- **What the SCREENER can and cannot do . . .**
- **What the GUARD can and cannot do . . .**
- **What the SCREENED PLAYER can and cannot do . . .**
- **What the REBOUNDER can and cannot do . . .**

And more. It's all there! In fact,

> **It would be very difficult to think of a contact situation that the rules committee hasn't already included in the Rules Book and/or the case book.**

Leaders of Officials, at all levels, whether they have ever officiated or not, must become **very knowledgeable** of the rules so they will **know** when their staff is, or is not, making **Accurate Rulings**—as opposed to just *"accepting each Official's personal judgment as good enough."* By the way, contact that was illegal fifty years ago is still illegal today. *"How long does it take us to learn them?"*

It now appears that the governing bodies of basketball have seen enough and have come to realize that . . .

> **The only way to achieve consistent accuracy is to rid officiating of anything that is being used as a substitute for learning and enforcing the Rules of THE GAME.**

Recently, the NCAA Men only had **one Point of Emphasis (P.O.E.):** *"Enforce the Rules As Written."* That same season, the NFHS's **#1 POE** was *"Enforce the Rules."* If these are the POE, one would have to ascertain, *"There must be a lot of Officials who are not enforcing the rules."* We all should be asking, *"Why not?"*

The **Officials' Code of Ethics** leaves us with no choice but to **Enforce the Rules** of **THE GAMES** we officiate. So with this **Code of Ethics** and with this well-written Rules Book, we each should be asking,

> *"Why would high school and college Officials have to be told after more than 120 years to enforce the rules that integrity requires them to enforce?"*

I'm sure we all know that integrity is certainly not the issue. Well, what is the culprit? Why the mandate requiring Basketball Officials to enforce the rules? Could it be that Officials have been taught to *"Trust Your Partner"* but never taught that it is okay to *"Trust the Rules"*?

PETER WEBB, Retired IAABO Coordinator of Interpreters, was recently quoted as saying, *"As I tour the IAABO states and some other states, we continue to see the same inaccurate rulings year after year. We have thirteen states that are not measuring up to the expectations of Basketball. IAABO, our Interpreters, Supervisors, Observers, and Officials need to care about it all, because it all matters!"*

One major general concern is the comingling of high school and collegiate Rules, Mechanics, and Signals. This is unacceptable! Peter went on to remind us,

"The expectations of our high schools as presented by the NFHS is that Officials who serve them bring the appropriate high school package of rules and officiating to their high school games." The rules are very clear regarding what is legal and what is illegal for A1 and B1, as well as their teammates. However, as stated previously, Officials can't make **Accurate Rulings** without **Accurate Rules Knowledge**. Officials and their leaders do not need to endeavor to *"figure out"* what is important or what does and does not matter. **It all matters! Learn it . . . Recognize it . . . Enforce it.**

As long as we have Officials, all across the country, who *"take it upon themselves"* to determine what contact is legal and what contact is illegal, instead of applying the **Rules**, we are not progressing, and games are filled with **Inaccurate Rulings**. Let's laugh again: *"He doesn't know the rules, but he has good judgment."*

Wise people can also listen and learn; even they can find good advice in these words.
—Proverbs 1:5

THE TONGUE IS ONLY
INCHES FROM THE
BRAIN, BUT WHEN
YOU LISTEN TO SOME
PEOPLE TALK,
MOUTH AND MIND
SEEM MILES APART.

CHAPTER 17

Stop Talking and Officiate

"Stop Favoring One Team over the Other."

Officials are great people, as a group, and they want to do the right thing. I have never encountered an incident where an Official was obviously cheating. The truth is, *"cheating"* is the exact opposite to what Sports Officials represent. We may be booed by biased fans, but if one of us were to actually *"cheat"* or be suspect to cheating, it would be National News.

During my twenty years of officiating at the DI level, we were required to watch a video at the Annual Fall Meeting on Gambling Crimes by players who received more than a Technical Foul when they were convicted. Some of these very poignant videos contained interviews from prisons, where the ex-college basketball players spoke of bad influences that were followed by bad choices. To see these terrific athletes, with tears streaming down their cheeks, will always be a vivid image to me. I hope such videos are required watching for all college basketball players now and in the future. I can only imagine the pain, embarrassment, and heartache these athletes felt when they left the courtroom and later heard those iron doors slam behind them, not to open for them again for seven to ten years.

> **Life is about choices; *"first we make choices . . . then those choices make us."***

There are life rules that society expects all its members to follow. When they do, all is well. When they don't, there are imposed penalties. The Courtroom Judge makes his/her Ruling based on the evidence. The Judge doesn't excuse the crime because the athlete only had one parent or due to the huge size of the bribe. The Judge hears the evidence and then penalizes.

The lawyers are totally different than the Judge. The Defense Attorney's job is to *"sell the Judge and Jury"* on the innocence of his/her client or some *"excusable justification"* for the crime. Often, the defendant is so obviously guilty, and the attorney simply *"pleads for mercy."*

The Judge and lawyers perform their duties while *"in"* the court, and Basketball Officials perform their duties while *"on"* the court. The purpose of this chapter's Topic is to more clearly characterize the Role of Game Officials as that of a **Judge** and not an Attorney, since Attorneys *"plead their case"* and Judges *"Make Rulings."* Be reminded of our Role as a Game Official:

> **Basketball Officials are to monitor the activity and then make rulings based on that activity. Doesn't that resemble the judge and not the lawyer?**

Too many Officials make efforts to be both due to their officiating *"upbringing."* They want to *"hold the hand"* of players to help them avoid getting caught for breaking the rules, thus helping them avoid committing violations and fouls. Often these noble efforts are referred to as *"preventive officiating."* I was *"raised on"* preventive officiating.

In another chapter, I mentioned the high-profile TV Official who told us in camp, ***"If you aren't talking ten players out of the lane in your game, you are not doing a good job of officiating."*** He did not invent such foolishness; he was just passing it on. This is an example of the Official who accepts the role of the *"attorney,"* and when that role doesn't work, he/she then becomes the *"Judge,"* who is the highest-ranked person in the gym.

> *"Game Officials are the judges . . . not the lawyers."*

One of the ongoing debates and *"arguments"* among Basketball Officials is **TO TALK OR NOT TO TALK.** To prevent or enforce. Officials who believe in *"talking players out of fouls or violations"* and offer *"warnings"* beyond what's allowed by rule continue to see themselves as something other than their true identity of a Game Official. They see themselves as the *"Lawyer"* on their court instead of the *"Judge"* who makes the final rulings. Perhaps you are one of the Officials, as I was, who was taught to prevent by talking. My goal here is for you to have a paradigm shift in your thinking and . . .

> **Stop the talking and start the enforcing.**

Let's compare the talkers and the nontalkers. To begin, we must ask ourselves, **"Why talk?"** As previously stated, the answer is clear: **to Prevent.** This causes us to ask, **"Why prevent?"** This question may get the *"Talking Officials"* excited and even defensive, as they, like I was, have been *"sold on this approach"* and truly believe that part of their role is to prevent as many fouls and violations as they can. This chapter is to *"talk"* you out of that approach, because it is clearly contrary to the Role of Game Officials and certainly contrary to anything that can be found in the Rules Book, Case Book and Officials Manual.

> **Why would we talk if they are playing legally? Why would we talk if they are playing illegally?**

The next question is, **"Why do we care if they foul or commit a violation?"** During my inquiries of many Officials, no Official ever had a quick responding answer to this question. I received more *"deer-in-the-headlight looks"* because no one had ever directed this question to them. Their weakly formulated answer was obviously coming from a *"lawyer Official"* whose response would not *"hold up in court."* Some answers to this ***"Why do we care?"*** question are excellent, convincing, and noble responses from Officials who care, who really work hard, and who desire to be the best Official they can be.

Let's go back to the first question and listen in on a Q and A Session between **THE GAME (The Judge of Accuracy)** and the *"talking lawyer-style Official."*

THE GAME. I heard you talking to the players during your game last night. Why were you doing that?

TALKING OFFICIAL. I was trying to talk them out of committing a foul.

THE GAME. Was there a foul?

TALKING OFFICIAL. No, Your Honor.

THE GAME. Was there contact?

TALKING OFFICIAL. Yes, sir, that's why I was talking to them.

THE GAME. Aren't you aware that I have Rules to cover all types of contact? If contact is illegal, then a foul has occurred. If the contact is legal, then there is no foul, and it is Incidental Contact. I'm confused as to why you would be talking on either of these. If there is a foul and you are talking instead of enforcing the Rules, then you and I need to talk. If you are talking during legal contact, where there is no foul and the Rules allow such contact, then I can't help but ask you again,

---

"Why are you talking and trying to stop legal contact?"

TALKING OFFICIAL. I was only trying to stop something that might happen if they continued the contact.

THE GAME. I see. That is a very noble gesture, but isn't that a warning?

TALKING OFFICIAL. Yes, sir, I suppose we can call it that.

THE GAME. So you are admitting to providing teams with more than the allotted warnings that are clearly listed in the Rules of my game?

TALKING OFFICIAL. When you ask it that way, I suppose you are right, but I was only trying to do what all the other Officials do and what we hear in camps, which is to try and prevent a foul if we can.

THE GAME. So they are actually teaching this nonsense in summer camps? Do you talkers get to choose which violations you want to prevent? Do you try to talk them out of Traveling, like you talk them out of the lane? Do you tell them to get their hands off instead of ruling a hand-checking foul and then rule the next hand check a foul because they didn't obey YOU? I suggest you rethink this approach, because I am not about YOU; I am about *ME*. Don't wait to see if they will obey *YOU*, when your job is to monitor and see if they will obey me and my rules. Shame on you! When they violate, a whistle should be heard. When they foul, a whistle should be heard.

THE GAME. Let me ask you another question, and maybe you can pass it on to your so-called trainers.

"Why do you care if there is a foul or a violation?"

THE GAME. Why does anyone care if A2 commits a three-seconds violation? Is each Official caring the exact same amount on both ends of the court? Again . . . can you share with me why Basketball Officials should be so fearful that a player will foul or violate that the Official would provide an illegal warning to the player?

THE GAME. Before you answer, let me ask you a specific violation question. If A1 were dribbling the ball up the court and barely step on the boundary line, would you warn him by telling him to be careful or you'll have to call that on him the next time? I'm just trying to understand just how far some of you Officials will go to avoid enforcing my rules.

TALKING OFFICIAL. Sir, we are being taught to see if we can help keep the star player in **THE GAME** because the fans did not come to see him/her sit on the bench.

THE GAME. One would think that the other team already knows who the star player is and have probably been working all week to minimize his/her contributions. And now . . . the Officials are going to join the star player's team by helping that player to stay out of foul trouble? I hope you know what that sounds like, and I further hope you don't like that sound!

> **"If the star player is so good, he or she should be able to play by my rules and not foul."**

THE GAME. Should you warn on the first block/charge collision by saying something like, "Are you guys okay? I didn't call anything that time, but I will the next time." Do you see how foolish that sounds? How do you think the players and coaches would react to such foolishness? Trust me, they'd be talking to you.

Talking Official. I have never thought of it that way, sir. That would be ridiculous.

THE GAME. You're right, and that's the way I feel when I see Officials trying to make me better when I don't need their help. They don't know how good it already is, because they won't enforce the rules all the time and stay out of the way with their preventive, caring mentality. Stop caring about anything except Accurate Rulings. That's it. That's your job! Make Accurate Rulings! When you choose to talk instead of enforcing the rules, you are not making accurate rulings, and you certainly are not helping me.

THE GAME. A talking Official is demonstrating a personal level of tolerance, and tolerance always favors one team over the other. Tolerance is always a personal thing, and any personal approach to officiating will always vary from one person to another. This causes the coach to ask questions like, "How are you guys calling hand checking tonight?" "How are you all calling three-seconds tonight?" etc. What is interesting to note is they never ask, "How are you guys calling out of bounds."

As you can see from the above discussion between **THE GAME** and the **Talking Official**, **THE GAME** makes some very good and solid points in an effort to get us to *"stop the talking"* and get back to our described Role of Officiating, which is to . . .

> **"Monitor the activity and enforce the rules that pertain to that activity."**

Here are some other thoughts on this subject, which I hope will cause you to say, *"Enough, Ray. I get it. I'm done talking. Let me move on to the next chapter for crying out loud!"*

What if you are a talker and your other Crew Members are not? What if you are a talker and tomorrow night's game Officials are not? The players are confused and often state, *"You didn't warn me first. Where's my warning?"* I have actually heard such.

When should you stop talking and start enforcing? The middle of the second quarter? The beginning of the second half? We've heard other talkers tell us to say, *"We can't be warning them in the fourth quarter,"* and *"Let us know when you warn a coach, so he/she doesn't get three warnings."* Not a bad idea, but what about hand checking? What about three seconds? What about hanging on the basket? Is your partner going to say to you, *"Keep an eye on number 21, and if he chins on the ring another time, let's get him"*?

When Basketball Officials *"stop caring"* and rid themselves of any hesitation that is brought on by the time on the clock or the score of **THE GAME**, then the fans will stop wondering if the Officials actually care who wins and who loses. Then the fans will stop wondering if we are *"part of the show"* like the Harlem Globetrotters Game Officials.

Talking to players to prevent a violation or to keep a player from being charged with a foul puts the Official in a position to say to the coach, **"Coach, I told him three times, but he wouldn't listen."** Somehow, this makes the Official feel justified when he/she finally does rule the violation or the foul because he/she has finally exhausted all available substitutes for enforcing the rules.

The communication process is not complete until everyone involved has seen and understood the delivered message, and that message is best delivered by Mr. Ron Foxcroft's awesome, black Fox 40 Whistle. It is all the *"talking"* that is needed, and it is the language that all players, coaches, and fans understand.

> *A person without wisdom enjoys being foolish, but someone with understanding does what is right.*
> —Proverbs 15:21

> TRUTH IS ALWAYS
> STRONG, NO MATTER
> HOW WEAK IT LOOKS, AND
> FALSEHOOD IS
> ALWAYS WEAK NO MATTER HOW
> STRONG IT LOOKS.
>
> —Antonius

CHAPTER **18**

Enough with the "Selling" Already!

"Remain Composed, Dignified, and Professional."

I'm sure we all agree that Basketball Officials are to always conduct themselves as Professionals, whether on or off the court, whether the ball is live or dead, whether the ruling is being booed or applauded. To state the obvious, Professionals are to conduct themselves professionally. A huge part of this behavior is composure. Composure is conducting oneself with dignity and pride, without getting excited, while acting as though one has seen this activity before now.

The *"act"* of *"selling one's rulings"* always includes a *"lack of composure"* and involves the use of unapproved and/or exaggerated signals and signaling. The Rules Book and the Officials Manual are very clear as to how Officials are to signal. Losing one's dignity while signaling improperly is not the expectation of basketball for its Officials.

There can be only one explanation for the *"act"* of *"selling rulings"* by any on-court Basketball Official. The explanation is simple: *"Convince others that you know you got it right."* *"Selling the calls"* has been around baseball for as long as there has been baseball, so it seems. I recall thinking as a child, *"Why does the umpire get so loud on Strike 3 but not on Ball 4?"* It always gives the impression and appearance that the Umpire is glad the batter struck out or the Official is glad A1 scored the goal for an *"And One."*

We all know that is not the case, because we Sports Officials couldn't care less as to which team wins or loses. We are the only ones on the field or in the gym who is unbiased; we don't care. With that being required and true, I say, **"Enough with the selling!"** It is not needed, not required, not necessary, and is certainly not sending the right messages to everyone involved in **THE GAME.**

QUESTION. *Why do Officials do it?*

ANSWER. They have been taught to do so.

QUESTION. *Who taught them to do so?*

ANSWER. Supervisors of Officials who taught them to convince the coach that they got it right.

When Officials are more concerned with *"pleasing the coach"* than *"pleasing THE GAME,"* we will always find them *"selling calls,"* *"talking instead of enforcing,"* and concerning ourselves with, *"What does the coach think?"*

This mentality of *"selling calls"* to convince the coach that your ruling was accurate became a *"required performance"* when we began having college supervisors of Officials who have never been Game Officials. In fact, many of these were, and still are, ex-coaches or Athletic Directors. They continue to have the mind-set of a coach and want to be *"sold"* on the Officials' rulings.

I am convinced that this *"selling"* practice of Officials demonstrates a certain type of *"fear"* of not being accepted, not having others believe in them, concern with what the coach may say, *"selling"* to avoid any discussion about the ruling. What would happen if we did not *"sell"* our rulings? Would you want to change it after talking with the coach? Would we appear weak? Would we appear unsure? Would we not be accepted? Trust me, *"selling our rulings"* will not change how the coach feels about us.

I wonder if we Officials would officiate the same way if the Head Coach were not allowed on the bench during **THE GAME.**

168

In other words, instead of being on the bench, the Head Coach had to be in an area like the Press Box, only to observe and see if his/her players were performing as they had practiced all week? What a great idea. Think about it. No confrontations. No Technical Fouls on the Head Coach and no need for going tableside after ruling a foul so you can talk to the Head Coach. Sounds interesting, huh? The Officials would not have to be concerned with *"what the coach thinks"* about anything. Again . . . ask yourself,

> *"Would I officiate differently if there were no head coaches allowed on the sideline?"*

Well, here is an *"accurate ruling"* for you: **That is exactly how we are to officiate!** When Officials are concerned with *"what the coach will think,"* then that Official can never be at his/her best any more than if he/she were officiating with a *"rock in one of his/her shoes."* That discomfort is a distraction. We can't be focused on our true assigned task when we are distracted or concerned with anything other than *"Monitoring the activity and making accurate rulings."* If you officiate for someone who mandates that you be demonstrative when signaling instead of demonstrating composure, then that is an obvious issue for you. Working for an untrained Basketball Official or some ex-coach who has never worn a striped shirt does indeed present some challenges. Perhaps this book would be a timely Christmas Gift from you to him or her.

> *"Can you imagine a college coaches' organization hiring a retired basketball Official to lead, direct, and impose mandates on college coaches? That will never happen. The reverse should never be allowed, either."*

By the way . . . while you're *"selling,"* you had better hope you have some *"buyers"*—especially now that every fan has a camera and the replay is shown many times on live television and YouTube.

Always remember: *"Selling an inaccurate ruling can never make it accurate."*

> *He that hath no rule over his own spirit is like*
> *a city that is broken down, and without walls.*
> *—Proverbs 25:28*

OFFICIATE SO YOUR
FRIENDS CAN
DEFEND YOU,
BUT NEVER NEED TO DO SO.

CHAPTER *19*

Always Consider Both Teams

"All Rulings Matter to Both Teams"
(Peter Webb).

One of the most important lessons I learned after being *"really trained"* by **PETER WEBB** was this: *"Always consider Both teams."* I was not *"raised in officiating"* to think that way. Until I began considering **both** teams, I was a *"talker;"* I was taught to be. Preventive Officiating was required—still is among many of us. When an Official really does begin to *"consider both teams,"* officiating becomes much easier. Less stressful. More fun and, certainly, more accurate.

Without rewriting a previous chapter, let me remind us that the culprit that favors one team over the other is a *"personal tolerance"* for illegal activity. This is another example of *"substitutes for rules enforcement."* This causes all of us to constantly be asking ourselves, *"When should I enforce 'that' rule?"* Do I enforce it after a warning? After two warnings? Which violations do I warn about, and which ones do I enforce immediately? Which contact am I going to consider to be a foul compared to my partners? Are they seeing the same game? Do they have some tolerance level that is not supported by the rules? Do I? Are they philosophical? And the *"stressful aspect of officiating"* continues while everyone involved in **THE GAME** keeps shaking their heads, trying to figure out *"why we ruled that way"* or *"why we didn't rule a certain way."*

In this chapter, we will discuss specific types of contact and what the Rules Book says about our rulings on these game situations.

The first area of concern is the **Contact** that takes place in the **backcourt**. As Team A is endeavoring to get the ball from backcourt to frontcourt status, we all must care about the **backcourt contact**, because to rule all contact in the backcourt as **incidental**, followed by a Ten-Second Violation is very *"weak and inaccurate officiating."* Backcourt contact must be judged the same as contact elsewhere. We must *"pay attention to"* and *"care about"* the Hand Checking, Arm Checking, and Body Checking (Bumping).

> **What** *we are seeing is* "nearly all contact is being treated as incidental, ***unless A1 loses the ball." This must change, as it simply cannot be condoned!***

WE NEED TO CARE MORE! IT ALL MATTERS!

Now the ball gets to the frontcourt where A1 is trying to **direct the offense** while being Hand Checked, Body Checked, Held, Bumped, Pushed, Hacked, and it appears his only *"prayer for a whistle"* is to *"cause the contact himself,"* hoping the Official rules in his favor.

WE NEED TO CARE MORE! IT ALL MATTERS!

When the ball gets loose and rolling on the floor, players are coached to *"Dive on the Ball!"* So the players **dive on** the ball, **dive at** the ball, and **dive on** each other. Observation gives the impression that Officials are *"putting their whistles in their pockets"* until someone gets control of the ball. It's like . . . anything goes!

Let's be reminded that *"contact that occurs when the ball is loose"* must be officiated the same as if the ball were not loose.

> **Just because the ball is loose does not entitle players to illegally contact an opponent by bumping, pushing, holding, or piling on.**

WE NEED TO CARE MORE! IT ALL MATTERS!

When the big player starts dribbling below the free throw line with his/her back to the basket, we can know that ***Bumping and***

Displacement are only seconds away. For the bigger player to dribble and bump, followed by more dribbling and more bumping that displaces the opponent and the sound of a whistle is not heard is an **Inaccurate Ruling** of illegal contact. **Displacement Contact** cannot be tolerated in schoolboy and schoolgirl basketball.

WE NEED TO CARE MORE! IT ALL MATTERS!

All contact rules are written for both the defense and offense. So when our friend A1 **causes** the contact by pushing off to *"create space"* to shoot the ball, we cannot rule this to be Incidental Contact but instead a **Player Control Foul**.

In addition, all too often, the Jump Shooter returns to the floor in the defender's space where contact occurs, and the defender is ruled for the foul. Let's be careful not to penalize the ***"Home Owner"*** for protecting himself when the *"intruder breaks into his house."*

WE NEED TO CARE MORE! IT ALL MATTERS!

It is crucial that Officials do not ***"follow the ball with their eyes,"*** instead of continuing to visually *"stay with the shooter"* after the release of the ball. If they visually follow the ball, they will have no knowledge of how A1 ended up on the floor or in the third row, following the shot. We must develop the excellent habit of ***"keeping our eyes on A1 and B1 but not concerning ourselves with whether the ball goes in the basket."***

Often, B1 makes a very good **Blocked Shot**, and the follow-through causes contact that is Incidental. However, when judging this contact, be sure to ***"stay with the matchup,"*** as the contact could move **from** incidental **to** illegal. As the play is being monitored, think of the potential consequences imposed on the shooter, such as affecting his/her ability to ***"Follow Your Shot"*** or ***"Get Back on Defense."*** In addition, we cannot allow contact on the shooter that causes him/her to *"not want to shoot anymore."* Or if they do, their next shot is unnatural or changed to avoid being the *"victim of such illegal contact"* that is ruled as legal.

WE NEED TO CARE MORE! IT ALL MATTERS!

Rebounding Contact calls for the Officials to know the difference between **over** the back and **on** the back and between **on** the back and ***"put on"*** the back. Careful and accurate monitoring will

175

clearly show if the contact involves **displacement**. If so, the correct and accurate ruling is a foul.

> **Just like the guard can OBTAIN and MAINTAIN, so can the rebounder. In fact, legal guarding position becomes legal rebounding position, simply by turning to face the basket— not facing the opponent. Now the rebounder can move to maintain that legal rebounding position, just as the guard can move to maintain the legal guarding position.**
>
> **And like the guard, when the rebounder is beaten, *"head and shoulders past head and shoulders,"* he/she is no longer in a legal maintaining rebound position.**

WE NEED TO CARE MORE! IT ALL MATTERS!

An Intentional Foul is defined in NFHS Rule 4, Section 19. The example given in Article 3c states (paraphrased), ***"Contact that is not a legitimate attempt to play the ball or player . . . is to be ruled as intentional. Contact that is specifically designed to stop the clock or keep it from starting is to be ruled as intentional . . ."***

Experienced Officials recognize that *"fouling is a coaching strategy,"* but that does not grant the Official *"permission"* to rule contact to be illegal when the same contact has been ruled as legal the entire game. Over the years, Officials have been taught to sound the whistle at the slightest touch because they know the defensive team wants the clock stopped. Not only does this *"approach"* violate **Rule 4.19.3c**; it demonstrates the Official has not considered the fact that . . .

> **The other team does not want the clock stopped. There are always two teams to consider!**

It is obvious that many Officials have been taught, ***"We better get the first one, or the next one could really be a hard one."*** Once again, Officials are not to get caught up in such thinking. We have rules that cover *"hard fouls."* Our role is not one of concerning ourselves with what the coach is doing. We are to *"**Monitor** the activities and **Enforce** the rules that pertain to that activity."*

WE NEED TO CARE MORE! IT ALL MATTERS!

Basketball Officials are the **Guardians** of **THE GAME** and much of what it stands for. We are charged with an awesome responsibility, and every time we walk out on the court, our goal cannot be *"consistency."* Striving for *"consistency"* causes Officials to make rulings on *"this end based on contact that occurred on the other end."*

> **Our goal is not consistency. Our goal should be consistent, accurate rulings.**

Basketball Officials are never to use *"**substitutes**"* for the Rules of **THE GAME**. We must officiate *"The Basketball Way."* Not my way or your way but *"The Basketball Way."* The IAABO motto is *"One rule, one interpretation,"* and I love it. However, it not only applies to violations but also to **Contact. Consistent, Accurate Contact Rulings** can only occur when those rulings are measured by what is clearly written in the **Rules Book** and **Case Book.**

WE NEED TO CARE MORE! IT ALL MATTERS!

The person with understanding is
always looking for wisdom, but the
mind of the fool wanders everywhere.
—Proverbs 17:24

**BEFORE YOU
CAN FINISH FIRST,
YOU MUST
FIRST FINISH.**

CHAPTER **20**

Every Game Has an Ending

"Our Role Is the Same Until the Final Horn Sounds."

> **Team A is leading by twenty points with four minutes remaining in the fourth quarter.**

Should the officiating be the same the last four minutes as it has been the first twenty-eight minutes? If not . . . what *"changes"* would we see in **THE GAME** you are officiating? Would we all be seeing the same *"necessary"* changes? Would we all be starting these changes at the same time of **THE GAME**? Would we all want to have the same score differential before beginning these changes? Here are some more *"Would you"* questions:

- Would you count slower?
- Would you count faster?
- Would you sound the whistle quicker?
- Would you delay even more before sounding the whistle?
- Would you allow the *"subs"* the same opportunity to perform as the starters?
- Would you hesitate to rule an obvious three-seconds violation on the team that is losing?

RAYMOND McCLURE

- Would incidental contact now be a foul for the purpose of stopping the clock?
- Would you hesitate to rule accurately on an obvious intentional foul?

WHAT YEAR WAS IT THAT SOMEONE FIRST SAID,
"Hey, let's officiate a little differently since the red team is so far behind"?
WHAT YEAR WAS IT THAT SOMEONE FIRST SAID,
"The rules of THE GAME are just a guideline"?
WHO WAS THE FIRST OFFICIAL WHO SAID,
"Let's not call that, since there's only two minutes to go in THE GAME"?
WHEN WAS IT THAT AN OFFICIAL FIRST SAID,
"All you need is good management skills and a feel for THE GAME"?
WHO WAS THE FIRST OFFICIAL TO PUT THE FANS BEFORE THE GAME BY SUGGESTING,
"Let's quickly recognize the best players and keep 'em in THE GAME"?
WHO WAS THE FIRST COACH WHO ASKED,
"How can you call that at a time like this"?
WHEN DID THE COACH FIRST ASK,
"How are you guys calling hand checking tonight"?
WHEN WAS IT THAT AN OFFICIAL FIRST SAID,
"Develop an officiating philosophy and use common sense out there"?
WAS IT A COACH OR AN OFFICIAL TO FIRST SAY,
"Let the Players Decide THE GAME"?
Who was the first supervisor to condone such end-of-game officiating?

"The supervisor's expectations will never exceed his/her explanations."

Based on observations at camps, state tournaments, and publications, today's Officials are obviously being taught to change the officiating when the score is lopsided, the time is running out, and/or the star player gets in foul trouble. We cannot support such officiating, because there is no Rules support or Manual support for such. That means **THE GAME** doesn't support such officiating either. Coaches and players may change how they perform but not us! We have no right! We don't care! We are **THE GAME Officials**!

The rules of **THE GAME,** and the **Role** of Officials remain the same throughout the entire game. It is **not** okay to *"look the other way"* in the fourth quarter. It is **not** okay to *"look for ways"* to avoid violations and fouls, such as counting too slowly, talking to players, or issuing *"warnings"* beyond the allotted four, which are allowed by rule.

There are always two teams to consider, and your personal tolerance level will always favor one team over the other. Stop trying to decide *"what matters"* because everything matters!

Accurate Rulings are always the requirement, and accuracy is always accurate, regardless of the time, the score, or the player with the ball. The Officials must **Honor THE GAME.** This is our required responsibility all the way to the end of **THE GAME.**

Efforts to please the coach or yourself instead of **THE GAME** is a disservice to the school and **THE GAME.** I recall hearing my MEAC Supervisor, Danny Doss, say during classroom training,

---

"I'd rather a coach be upset at me for enforcing a rule . . . than not enforcing it."

The urgency of situations may change and intensify for the teams near the end of **THE GAME** but not for us. The **Role** of the Officials remains the same throughout the entire game. A team may want to stop the clock, but the rules regarding contact do not change near the end of **THE GAME.** Rules enforcement can't be affected due to the score or time remaining. Is *"fouling on purpose"* a coaching strategy? Absolutely. However, the contact must be a foul, just as it has been earlier in **THE GAME**.

Well, *"we better get the first one, or the second one could be intentional or a fight."* This mentality should not be any concern to Officials. We have **RULES** to cover Intentional Fouls and Fights. The Officials are to be dignified, professional, well-trained, and always composed while officiating **THE GAME** by the rules all the way to the very end.

> *"It is a shame that the toughest part of officiating is trying to decide 'when' to enforce a rule."*

Let's not *"kick these rules"* because one team wants the clock stopped:

- **Ruling a foul on contact that has been incidental earlier in THE GAME**
- **Granting a time-out to the scoring team after the other team already has team control for their throw-in**
- **Ruling a common foul that is obviously an intentional foul**

Always consider *"the other team;"* they probably don't want the clock stopped.

I recognize that some readers will choose not to *"buy into"* this type of *"end-of-the-game officiating."* I didn't either, at first. However, we have no choice when we choose to always honor the high school game. One of the many *"lifelong lessons"* we all want the student athletes to learn is *"choices have consequences"* even in the last two minutes of a lopsided game.

THE GAME is not over when the final horn sounds. In fact, by Rule, the final score is not approved until all Officials leave the visual confines of the playing area. To leave the court too soon, especially in a very close game, could result in the wrong team being declared the winner. A good technique is to meet in the Center Restraining Circle at the end of any *"close game."* The suggested definition of a *"close* *game"* is four points or less. From this vantage point, the Referee can receive a *"thumps-up"* signal from the Official Scorer, informing the Referee that there are no scoring issues and it is now okay to leave the court. When you do leave the court, leave as a crew—together.

> **Do not exit as though you just stole something, but leave as a professional who has just completed a service to the school. In addition, remember to go directly to the dressing room. No delays. No visiting. No talking to each other until behind closed doors.**

The dressing room is a very private room, and only the Crew is allowed there. Just as a Pregame Conference is necessary, so is a Postgame Conference. Granted, this conference will normally not last as long as the Pregame Conference, as it is private time to quickly review **THE GAME.** Talk about the accuracy of the rulings throughout **THE GAME.** Double Whistles, Officiating Teamwork, Technical Fouls, Intentional Personal Fouls, along with anything else that is *"fresh on the minds"* of the entire crew.

Be sure to exit the facility together as a Crew of Officials. Is Security Personnel necessary? Available? Our attitude regarding our *"other friends"* in uniform (Security Personnel) is always one of respect, gratitude, and appreciation. We always should want them there. Be a handshaker. Be sincere. Smile and say *"hello"* and *"good night."* They, too, are there to serve, and one of their main responsibilities is our safety. Make sure they know you appreciate them.

If you stop at the local sports bar/restaurant for your postgame glass of milk, be aware that you have entered the premises that have ended the careers of Officials over the years. Be very careful what you say and how loudly you speak, and never forget that *"someone is always listening and watching."*

This is another excellent opportunity to demonstrate professional behavior in language, choice of beverages, and subject matter of conversation. Again . . . remember, ***"The microphone is always on."***

So, as another reminder, the Rules of **THE GAME** do not change even though the score is lopsided, and neither does the **Role** of the Officials. The **rules are nonnegotiable truths.**

Respect, trust, honor, and comply with the decisions of the rules committee; and trust the rules all the way to the end of THE GAME!

They rejected my advice and paid no attention when I corrected them. Therefore, they must eat the bitter fruit of living their own way, choking on their own schemes.
—Proverbs 1:30–31, NLT

I'M GOING TO STOP
ASKING, "HOW
DUMB CAN YOU GET?"
SOME PEOPLE SEEM TO BE
TAKING IT AS A CHALLENGE.

CHAPTER **21**

"Ticky-Tack" Fouls

"There Is No Such Thing."

All too often, we read or hear someone who is perceived as an *"expert"* make a statement like this: ***"Don't be out there calling ticky-tack fouls."*** Have you ever wondered what such a *"Training Tip"* is endeavoring to accomplish? My guess is we know what is trying to be taught; however, it is time for Writers, Trainers, Interpreters, and Supervisors to *"write and speak accurately"* so the Trainee can immediately learn and apply these *"quick, short lessons."*

The purpose of this short chapter is to increase the awareness of the importance of writing and speaking with **Rules Book Terminology** every time we write or speak. Basketball Officials are the Professionals of **THE GAME**, which requires us to use the *"real language"* of **THE GAME**. Nowhere do we find *"ticky-tack"* in any of our support materials, such as the **Manual**, **Rules Book**, or **Case Book**. The truth is, *"ticky-tack"* is in the same category as *"be strong"* . . . *"work hard"* . . . *"pass on it"* . . . *"call the obvious,"* etc.

Have you ever heard someone reference **"ticky-tack"** violations? Probably not. Can you imagine a Clinician making a statement such as ***"That was a ticky-tack call. He barely stepped on the sideline,"*** or ***"He barely traveled,"*** ***"She barely double dribbled."*** Sounds humorous, doesn't it? To the thoroughly trained and caring Basketball Official, such references to **contact** are just about as humorous. To officiate or train Officials in this manner is really, shall we say, *"ticky-tack."*

As has been stated in nearly every chapter so far, we have too many Officials and Leaders of Officials who officiate and train as though **violations** are to be officiated by the Rules while **contact** is to be officiated by *"something else."* **This is wrong! The Rules are very clear** as to what contact is **Legal** and what contact is **Illegal**. Therefore, **there is no such thing as a *"ticky-tack"* foul**, because the contact was, by **Rule**, either Legal or Illegal; and the Ruling was either **accurate** or **inaccurate** based on the rules.

By the way, it saddens me to say that it was reported to me in the summer of 2015, by text, from a camp classroom, that the then Supervisor of the Men's Officials for that major DI Conference was quoted as saying, *"You guys have got to stop calling those incidental travelings."* Shocking, huh? Do you think the Officials' Supervisor of any other sport would dare make such a statement of dishonor regarding the rules of their sport?

In addition, there is no such thing as a *"marginal call."* There are **no rules** that can be accurate **two** ways, such as *"That one could have gone either way."* No, it couldn't have! The Ruling, every time, was either **accurate** or **inaccurate** based on the written **rules** of **THE GAME**.

Supervisors must hold Officials accountable for their rulings, instead of just saying, *"Well . . . that's Ray's judgment."*

Ray's judgment is either **accurate judging** or **inaccurate judging**, based on **the rules**. If Ray's judging is consistently wrong, Ray should be trained before he returns to the court. By the way, and to repeat, *"Selling"* an **inaccurate ruling** never makes it **accurate**.

We all should remove the mentality of *"I passed on that."* We Officials **never pass on anything**. We **always** make a **ruling**, and sometimes the sound of a whistle can be heard. When there is no whistle, the Official ruled the activity as being **legal**. If the activity was actually **illegal** and the Official did not penalize that **illegal** activity, the Official made an **inaccurate ruling**. He/she *"kicked a rule"* by not sounding the whistle.

Too many very good Officials do officiate by the Rules, but some think it is their *"personal approach"* or their *"personal judgment."* It is time for all Officials, especially the quality ones, to *"admit"* they are a **rules expert**, and they will **honor THE GAME** by enforcing the Rules as written. If they are **not** a Rules Expert, one must, once again, ask,

> *"How long does it take? How many years does it take to learn sixty-eight pages of anything?"*

Doctors do brain surgery after twelve years' experience, and we can't get block/charge right after **TWELVE YEARS! TWENTY YEARS! THIRTY YEARS! ONE HUNDRED AND TWENTY-FIVE YEARS!**

Well-trained Officials know Rule 4.27 (Incidental Contact), and that causes them to know the difference between **Legal** contact and **Illegal** contact. The *"issue"* is many of these Officials want to call it *"game management"* or a *"feel for THE GAME."* Instead, they should refer to it as **Rules Enforcement** and admit,

> *"I know the rules, and I enforce the rules, because I have no choice. It is my job. It is what I get paid to do. I am a game Official, and my shirt tells the world that I am a person of integrity and character who would never intentionally fail to enforce a game rule."*

I say this so that no one can fool
you by well-crafted arguments
that seem good but are false.
—Colossians 2:4

**IF YOU CONTINUE TO DO WHAT'S RIGHT,
WHAT'S WRONG AND WHO'S WRONG
WILL EVENTUALLY LEAVE YOUR LIFE.**

CHAPTER **22**

Don't Forget to Learn the Last Rule

"Especially the Last Two and a Half Pages"

Can you imagine, as a student, receiving a book assignment and then failing to read the last chapter? You wouldn't know how it ended. When you made your book report, you'd have to either guess at the ending or simply make it up; neither of which would have a good chance at being accurate. However, you could get by with your book report as long as your teacher has never read the book. Taking such liberties and being creative with your *"unique ending"* could be very risky. The risk is about fifty-fifty as to whether your teacher is familiar with the end of the book and how the story actually ends. I strongly suggest that we finish the task and read all the way to the end of the book so our *"book report"* will be an accurate one, thus eliminating the *"need"* to be creative in our readings.

One of the most frustrating things in life for someone of my personality is *"unfinished tasks."* I'm just *"wired that way."* It is not always a good thing and has caused me confrontational moments when I was dumb enough to point them out. In some cases, people like me are often seen as being too critical or *"sticking their nose where it doesn't belong."* Probably true in most cases. These unfinished tasks remind me of the time I set my DVR to record a basketball game so I could watch it when I got home. We've all done that, right? However, not planning for **THE GAME** to go into overtime, the recorder stops before the end of **THE GAME**. Now I must go online to get the final score without seeing the exciting ending. An *"unfinished task"* never fails to frustrate.

We drive through the neighborhood and see an unfinished mowed lawn. We bring our dog from the groomer, and they obviously did not take pride in their work with our pup. Your teenager is told to clean her room before she goes out, but she left before the clearly defined task was completed. This list could go on, and on and perhaps you have a *"pet peeve"* that comes to mind as you also think of an incomplete performance.

This short chapter is to remind each game Official of the tremendous importance of the *"end of the Rules Book."* By the time the new Official gets this far along in the Rules Book, he/she has already read about Contact back in Rule 4, where various types of Contact are defined, such as guarding, screening, blocking, incidental contact, etc. When the Official gets to Rule 10 Section 6, the Head Coach's Rule, stories break out about technical fouls on the Head Coach, and the Official fails to learn Rule 10.7. Well, at least it appears that way too often when observing Officials' on-court performance.

The emphasis here is on **Rule 10 Section 7** because without an absolute and thorough knowledge of this Rule,

> **The contact rulings by a group of Officials or any two Officials will never achieve the goal of consistent, accurate rulings.**

The Officials' knowledge will vary on *"what is legal"* and *"what is illegal"* contact. The end result becomes **inconsistent** officiating, leaving the fans, coaches, and even partners *"scratching their heads in wonder"* as to **why** that contact was ruled a foul or **why** that contact was ruled as legal play.

One of the main themes throughout this book, and certainly the ultimate goal here, is to teach that **Consistent, Accurate Rulings** can be the norm. And as stated previously, Officials must learn that Violations **and** Contact must be officiated by the **Rules**. Yes, by the Rules. Trying to officiate Violations by the Rules and contact by *"something else"* is one of the main culprits that causes inconsistencies and inaccuracies.

> **Rule 10.7 has been written with very clear wording as to what contact is legal and what is illegal.**

The key to learning this Rule is to read and study it often. Very often. Then it becomes clear, and the reader realizes that the player who **Causes** the Contact is the player who is to be charged with the foul. Some of these **Causes** are listed all the way back in Rule 4.23 and 24. Other **causes** are specifically listed in the Screening (Rule 4.40) and Verticality (Rule 4.45) Rules; these are then clarified in Rule 10.7. The wording is so intentionally clear that the Official will not be wondering, ***"What does that mean?"***

The effect of the Contact has always been the *"measuring stick"* in which to determine if the Contact were legal (incidental) or illegal (foul). Advantage versus Disadvantage is often the determining factor as to whether we hear a whistle.

> **By the way . . . Officials are never to use advantage/disadvantage when making violation rulings.**

Rule 10, Section 7 *"gave birth"* to a new Article at the beginning of the 2014-2015 NFHS season—a new *"last chapter"* in the Rules Book. This new addition to the Rules Book now mandates that the covering Official will no longer get to consider the *"effect"* of certain types of listed Contact by the defender on a player in control of the ball. This *"certain contact"* is to be ruled a foul, whether the monitoring Official believed the Contact to be a foul or not. Due to the ever-growing amount of *"acceptable contact"* by the contemporary Officials, the Rules Committee felt it necessary to *"spell it out"* for **THE GAME** Officials so the *"same contact"* would always be ruled as illegal. If that is what it takes to *"cause"* **Consistent, Accurate Rulings**, then so be it. Thus, **Rule 10.7.12.**

What is interesting to note is the Rules for other Contact are also just a clearly written, leaving the covering Official with no personal choice when making the ruling. No personal *"feel for THE GAME."* No personal tolerances allowed. Either the Screen was legal or illegal, **by the written rule**. The contact during all Block/Charge rulings is either legal for the player in control of the ball or illegal, **by the written rule**. The same applies to every other Contact situation during all basketball games.

As stated elsewhere in several places among these pages, The Rules Book declares that . . .

> *"The Player Shall NOT . . ."*
> *"The Dribbler Shall NOT . . ."*
> *"The Defender Shall NOT . . ."*
> *"The Rebounder Shall NOT . . ."*
> *"The Screener Shall NOT . . ."*

Then we game Officials are obligated and shall **NOT** fail to penalize this illegal activity, regardless of the time, the score, how one *"feels,"* or which player has the ball.

We Officials must accept the fact that if a player while dribbling the ball steps on a boundary line, that player is out of bounds. Clearly written, huh? This is illegal activity, **by the written rule**. A very easy and accurate ruling, right? No warnings. No options to consider. Obvious violation. If the covering Official rules this as legal activity, then the Official has *"kicked a rule."* We don't like to *"kick rules,"* do we? Now take this same approach when learning Contact. **Learn the Rules that pertain to Contact**, just as well as you know the rules for violations, and it will become much easier for all of us to reach our goal of **Consistent, Accurate Rulings**. So constantly read and study to become an expert on all the Rules of **THE GAME**.

194

That can only happen when you *"master" the* last two and a half pages.

A student is not better than the teacher,
but the student who has been fully
trained will be like the teacher.
        —Luke 6:40 (Words of Jesus)

**FOR MOST OF US,
OUR BEST FRIENDS ARE THOSE WHO
UNDERSTAND OUR
PAST, BELIEVE IN OUR FUTURE, AND
ACCEPT US TODAY.**

CHAPTER **23**

Natural-Born Basketball Official?

"Artist or Learned Skill?"

After college, I taught school in Peoria, Illinois, however, for only one year. During the summer following that first year of teaching, I was hired to be an insurance salesman for W. Clement Stone's Combined Insurance Company of America, located in Chicago. This proved to be an awesome experience for me, and I shall always be grateful for the many lessons learned in this *"commission only"* form of employment.

The training at Combined Insurance was so precise and detailed that we stayed in a Chicago hotel for two weeks. Yes, two full weeks away from home to ensure we had the necessary tools and skills to perform our assigned tasks. This truly was an amazing ***"Success System That Never Fails"*** (the title of one of Mr. Stone's Books).

I was so *"committed to success"* that I knew the Sales Presentation and every possible rebuttal *"word-for-word."* I was taught to use emphasis, hesitation, modulation, and humor, during the entire Seven-Minute Sales Presentation. I had been trained by the best the company had to offer during those fourteen consecutive days and nights at the Home Office and the hotel located on Sheridan Road on Chicago's north side. I was trained and ready to go out into the world and sell *"a promise to pay"* (insurance) to strangers.

I recall an interesting statement made by one of my favorite Motivational Speakers, the late-great Zig Ziglar, when he said, and I paraphrase,

> "*I* have never seen an ad in the newspaper announcing that a 'salesman' was born; or an actor, doctor, or teacher was born; only babies were born. *H*owever, I have seen *announcements for the funerals of salesmen, funerals for actors, doctors, and teachers. Therefore, somewhere between their birth and their death, they had to get trained in their chosen profession.*"

In 1984, I became a business partner with one of the best portrait Artist I have ever known. Paul Miller was awesome. In fact, he was so good he was commissioned by a local Republican Party Group to create a *"storytelling"* montage painting of the life of then President Ronald Reagan. It was a beautiful painting and certainly one of my favorites, with the title, ***"Profile of a Leader."*** Paul and I were partners for ten years, as he would use his amazing God-Given Talents to create *"history telling"* images, unlike anything ever seen. He was an Artist, and I was a Salesman. We really did have an awesome business arrangement for us both, as we sold millions of dollars of his art prints over our years together.

One would think that some of his talents would have *"rubbed off on me"* during our partnership. We had discussions, I watched him paint; I even tried it myself, but it proved to be a *"waste of time."* I simply did not have the *"artist"* in me. I am not *"wired that way."* The truth is, I found it most difficult to even paint a straight line, and when one can't do that, even *"stick men"* get offended by the efforts.

My point in writing this chapter is this:

> ***"There is a huge difference between a learned skill and a natural ability to create."***

Of course, there are Art Schools where Artists go to learn, but they are building on something that is already there in their

"DNA"—a natural artistic talent. These are *"Creative"* individuals; they just have it, while others, like me, don't.

Only certain individuals can sculpt, because they already see the image inside the stone, and all they are doing is removing the excess rock or ice from around *"what they already see."* All of us can't do that. Only Artist can.

When Basketball Officials are taught that they are to be an *"artist,"* that is sending an inaccurate description of *"what it takes to succeed"* in this avocation. It resembles that of teaching a Bartender that he/she must first be an artist. Or a Plumber. Electrician. These are skilled laborers who have been **trained**, who have **learned** their trade, and who know how to perform their tasks to the satisfaction of their customers.

> **These skilled workers do not see themselves as artists, and neither should basketball Officials.**

I'm sure most individuals who use the term *artist* are using it in a noble effort to assist Basketball Officials in the development of better *"people skills."* When I recognize a trainee who is an excellent communicator, he/she immediately *"stands out"* as one who may develop more quickly as an Official. Excellent Basketball Officials do have terrific *"people skills,"* and that is certainly a plus. A good communicator who is properly trained as an Official has a much better chance at being accepted and successful than one who has a personality that *"brightens up a room"* . . . when he walks **out**. We know that Head Coaches are emotionally involved in their coaching, and they see everything through biased eyes. Officials who are excellent communicators with good people skills and a thorough knowledge of the rules will know how to communicate effectively with Coaches to keep them focused on their role of coaching. Rule 10 is very clear regarding bench personnel behavior, and the Head Coach is a *"member"* of the bench personnel. Communicating effectively and professionally can often keep the Head Coach from violating the Head Coach's rules. There should be no substitutes for Rules Enforcement.

Basketball Officials must be trained properly with a foundation upon which to build a successful career. The best ones will learn the Rules and enforce them without being swayed or influenced by the time on the clock, the score, or which player has the ball. In addition, just as any skilled occupation requires certain physical capabilities, so does officiating basketball games. A blind plumber is not going to be our first choice to fix a leaking faucet, and neither would we consider hiring someone who could not climb a ladder to solve our roofing problem. The point is, to state the obvious, there are certain required physical attributes necessary to perform certain skills.

> **However, we continue to hear trainers repeating the same *"stuff"* they were taught, and it simply doesn't make the basketball Official better at being a basketball Official.**

Today's Basketball Officials are excellent at the things they are *"not asked to do by basketball"* while obviously lacking at the required and clearly defined role of a well-trained Basketball Official. Someone who has influence, please *"step up to the plate"* and simply demand *"accountability for accuracy"* because nothing should be allowed to be a *"substitute for accuracy."* Not ignorance of Rules, not bad eyesight, not being too slow to use proper coverage, not some *"feel for* **THE GAME**,*"* and certainly not *"situational officiating."*

Not everyone can be an *"Artist,"* because it takes more than physical qualities; it takes a creative mind. One doesn't need to be *"creative"* to become an acceptable Basketball Official. In fact, creativity should be discouraged. There is no need for us to try to resculpt it, repaint it, redesign it or recreate it.

> **It is already a beautiful finished product that is losing its beauty and appeal due to Officials and others trying to *"leave their mark"* by chiseling away very vital signals, mechanics, and rules that are the backbone of THE GAME.**

It resembles gang-related graffiti on a beautifully created bridge. To that, I respectfully remind us that **THE GAME** has already been created and the Role of Officials is to Officiate by *"monitoring the activity and enforce the rules pertaining to that activity."*

The best *"Art of Officiating"* is to become an expert of the Rules and then enforce them while using Proper Mechanics and Approved Signals. In addition, become an excellent communicator with good people skills, and leave the *"creativity"* to those who are *"real artist"* and who can create something that is new and not already more than 125 plus years old.

> *"Poets are artists, and poetry demands variety. Officiating doesn't want variety. It wants accuracy and the proper performance."*

Whatever your hand finds to do,
do with all your might.
—Ecclesiastes 9:10

THE ROAD TO
SUCCESS IS ALWAYS
UNDER
CONSTRUCTION.

CHAPTER **24**

The Rules of the Road

"What Is the Spirit and Intent of a Stop Sign?"

My minor in college was Traffic and Safety, as I aspired, at that time, to teach Driver's Education, along with my Coaching. This took some of my friends by surprise, as I have always been an *"aggressive driver,"* which is one of the habits we would teach our students to avoid. My Degree came from Illinois State University, and my Student Teaching was at Morton High School, located not too far from Peoria, there in Illinois.

The training I received from the Courses I took has really served me well over these many years and probably has saved my life a time or two. How many times have I said to myself, *"Whoa, I'm sure glad I head checked before changing lanes?"* The truth is, I *"mastered"* many really good driving habits and continue to use them today. My real driving weakness, which I discouraged in my children and students, is the aggressive *"conquer the trip"* mentality. If the speed limit is 55, I never have seen any reason to take a long time to get up to that limit. ☺ As I write this book, I am closing in on driving more than two million miles in my lifetime, thanks to a life of sales, playing Senior Softball and officiating basketball. I recall telling my dad, a Minister, not to worry, as I always have God as my copilot. His response was quick with, *"You'd better let him out before you kill him."* He was funny that way, which is one of the many things I miss about him.

> *Driving a vehicle is a very serious task that requires much skill. The same is true for basketball officiating.*

Learning to drive a vehicle on public roads should not be learned at the expense of occasional accidents, causing loss of life, limb, or property. A well-educated, properly trained driver is the kind of driver you'd rather face on a wet road as your oncoming traffic. I am convinced that Driver's Education Classes being removed from our public schools has been one of the poorest and most damaging decisions ever made for our children.

Our firstborn child is Connie Rene McClure Lawson, who has certainly brought much pride and joy to our hearts from the first day she *"discovered this planet."* It sure seems the pages of life turned very fast, and right after her sixteenth birthday, she and I were pulling into the Driver's License parking lot of Cobb County Georgia. She was an awesome and beautiful young lady who absolutely knew she was ready to put that magic little card in her purse so she could borrow the car whenever the opportunity presented itself.

Having a father who is well trained in this field of *"Traffic and Safety"* was sure to be an advantage over the other teens there for the same reason. She was ready to breeze through the hassle of driving in a parking lot without knocking over some red cones. Of course, I was drilling into her head and constantly reminding her all the way out there to come to a complete stop, use the Turn Signal Lights, and turn into the nearest lane that is going into the direction you will be traveling. She was ready, and we both knew it.

The Uniformed Officer immediately proved to be the kind of person who would brighten up a room . . . when she walked **out**. To learn that she had ever smiled in her life would have taken Connie and me by surprise. Anyway . . . Connie is smart, well-behaved, and certainly prepared. As they pulled away from the curb to begin the driving exam, I recall how proud I was of this wonderful young lady and how nervous I was for her.

They proceeded from the curb to the first stop sign, where I saw the left-turn signal come on, which caused on *"Atta, girl"* to sneak out of my mouth. Now to the stop sign and the left turn. Did I say **STOP** sign? You know that big red octagon road sign? My wife's daughter rolled through that sign and did **not** stop. In addition, she turned into the oncoming traffic lane, instead of the closest lane going in the direction she was to go. I learned a few minutes later that the Driving Instructor immediately told her to *"Drive back over to your daddy."* Yes, she had quickly failed her first try at acquiring the prized possession of a Driver's License. When I asked her if she wanted to drive home, her response was a very quick and frustrated, *"NO!"* Obviously, she was successful on her second try a few weeks later and has been driving ever since. Connie learned her lesson regarding stop signs and lane usage without anyone getting hurt or any auto accidents. She was not learning at the expense of anyone or anything.

Oh, for Basketball Officials to learn the same way.

The first three words of Ephesians 5:15 are *"BE VERY CAREFUL . . ."* In the original language, this admonition is much stronger than what a mother might say to her children as they go outside to play. These three words describe a *"way of living"* that is precise, accurate, and deliberate. It involves foresight and an enhanced awareness, like the way you should drive a car. You need to be constantly attentive, ready to respond to every possible situation that occurs. You must be ready to swerve to avoid hazards and brake for pedestrians while following the Rules of the Road.

Every decision you make while driving a vehicle requires skill, knowledge, and an awareness that is uninterrupted. All decisions must be wise, accurate, and well-prepared responses.

Oh, for Basketball Officials to be so prepared.

When Basketball Officials hold **THE GAME** in high esteem, they will honor it, protect it, and defend it, as any Guardian would do. Connie learned crucial lessons on the Driving Course where no one was at risk of injury or loss. Officials must do the same. We must stop allowing Officials to learn this trade *"at the expense of THE GAME."* Learning the Rules of the Road before getting on the road seems to be the logic order of things, and so does learning the Rules of basketball before getting on the court.

Obviously, knowing the *"Rules of the Road"* doesn't make one an excellent driver; neither does scoring a perfect grade on a basketball rules exam make one an excellent or desirable Game Official. Being skilled enough to maneuver the vehicle is crucial, and that skill increases with experience—lots of driving experience. Knowing how to apply the learned knowledge and enforce the rules of basketball in a timely manner also requires much experience. The latter is only taught and learned on the court and probably always will be. However, to put Officials on the court before they prove a thorough knowledge of the Basic Rules of basketball creates a situation of *"learning at the expense"* of **THE GAME**. This approach can easily be avoided, and it should be.

Learn the four foundational topics first . . . the rules second . . . the approved signals third, and proper mechanics fourth. Then learn how to officiate!

When this has been completed, the Official can now learn how to officiate basketball games without as much risk to **THE GAME**. In addition, the proper Foundation has been created upon which to build a solid officiating career. IAABO figured this out more than ninety-five years ago.

Back to the highway. Should all the Rules of the Road be obeyed? All the time? Only when a Police Officer is present? Only when other vehicles are present? Only when your children are in the car with you? Just asking.

Back to the basketball court. Should all the Rules of **THE GAME** be enforced? All the time? Only when your Supervisor or Assignor is watching? Only when the score is close? Only in the first half? Only when it *"bothers"* you? Just asking.

When driving a car from point A to point B, **if the goal** is to arrive without an accident occurring and that is accomplished, then . . .

> **It really doesn't matter if the driver used good driving habits or followed the rules of the road.**

Whether you signaled before turning or changing lanes doesn't matter. Whether you turned into the nearest lane going in your direction or not doesn't matter. Whether you exceeded the speed limit or not doesn't matter. Whether you came to a complete stop at stop signs or ran red lights . . . doesn't matter. What matters is that you arrived at Point B. You successfully reached your goal.

Using this same thought process, too many Officials are officiating basketball games with the same mentality, as we often hear them say, *"None of that stuff matters, as long as we get the call right."* Officials who share this mentality are not the Officials you want to run up and down the court with you in a close game, with time running out, because too often the wrong team will win **THE GAME**. Just as bad drivers on the road are easy to spot, so is it with Officials who share this mind-set of *"just get the call right."* They don't count in the backcourt, they stand with hands on hips during free throws and don't count, they rarely designate the throw-in spot, they like to talk instead of enforcing, etc. You get the idea.

Everything drivers do when behind the wheel is important. That's why they must have an uninterrupted focus when driving. No texting. No eating. No drinking. No looking for things you dropped. Uninterrupted concentration. Uninterrupted focus on the task at hand.

> **Oh, for Basketball Officials to be so focused. So caring.** *"Everything matters!"*

When you think about it, our best drivers should be our young people. Just think they have better eyesight, quicker reflexes, clearer minds, etc. However, it is not until they reach the age of twenty-five until their (our) insurance rates get reduced, assuming they have been a *"good student"* of the road. Why is that? The first word that comes to mind is *experience* or the lack of it. Even though they may have the best physical qualities and look as though they are our best drivers, they are not. Everyone knows this except the teenage drivers themselves. Until they have experienced and survived near misses, road rage, hydroplaning, icy conditions, bad wipers, following too closely, etc., they are really lacking in the crucial and necessary moments called experience.

I urge our schools to bring back Driver's Education Classes for their students, so they are properly prepared before merging onto the highways and the byways of our roads, streets, and avenues. Dodging cones and parallel parking in a Driver's License parking lot does not resemble what really goes on out there on the highways and city streets.

> **I also urge our high schools to demand proof that their varsity coaches know the rules of THE GAME they will be teaching their students.**

When they do, they, too, will know if the ruling of the Official is accurate or not . . . by Rule. I repeat, IAABO figured this out more than ninety-five years ago.

In addition, as Basketball Officials, let's hold each other accountable for the Training Programs and get serious about having our Officials prove they are very knowledgeable of the Rules, Mechanics, and Signals before ever officiating a Varsity Game. That doesn't mean they must know it all, but it does mean they can score very high on a closed-book exam and a floor test during subvarsity games. They will make mistakes and even rule inaccurately on some violations and contact, but it won't be due to a lack of knowledge, rather a lack of experience.

Please don't teach them to learn the *"Spirit and Intent"* of the Rules, because we don't know where to send them to learn them. Perhaps the *"Spirit and Intent"* of the Rules of Basketball are just as clear as the *"Spirit and Intent"* of a **STOP SIGN**. The meaning is not left to anyone's personal interpretation, personal or group philosophy, personal judgment, or even a unique *"feel."* No. The Stop Sign says what it means. It doesn't suggest we yield or slow down; it commands the drivers to **STOP**.

> **The instruction and meaning of a stop sign is very clear, and so are the rules of THE GAME.**

Don't let anyone capture you with empty philosophies and high-sounding nonsense . . . "
—Colossians 2:8

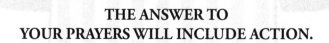

**THE ANSWER TO
YOUR PRAYERS WILL INCLUDE ACTION.**

CHAPTER **25**

For Better or Worse

"Honor and Respect THE GAME Like You Should Your Spouse."

Marriage is a sacred act of love, honor, and commitment. It should be entered after much prayer and consultation with a Minister or personal spiritual guidance counselor. I strongly recommend a thorough study of the Bible on this topic before pledging one's life to another. The Bible is very clear on this *"rule,"* just as the Rules Book is equally clear on what is a violation and a foul. Yes, I am one of those Churchgoing, Bible-Toting Believers who is certainly *"not perfect but definitely forgiven."*

Many marriages end in divorce for various reasons, and there are always *"two sides"* of the breakup story. Was it her fault, or did he cause it? Did the couple ever really love one another? Did they like one another? Were they best friends? Were they compatible? These, and many other questions, may be answered, and the real reason for the divorce may surface, but at the root of the cause, we will usually find that one or both stopped honoring and stopped dating the other. Did they stop saying, *"Thank you"* and *"Please"*? Did they stop holding hands? When did he stop opening the door for her? When did he begin walking ahead of her in public and leave her walking alone behind him? When did she become a nagger, complainer, whiner, or nonsupporting of his interest? Like I stated, there are always *"two sides."*

Keeping the friendship and affection alive is the key, and that requires an ongoing effort from each spouse. This behavior keeps the affection, respect, and honor for your mate alive. We should never treat our spouse or behave around our spouse in a manner that we would not do in the presence of guests in our home.

As you can already ascertain, I am not a Marriage Counselor, but I am a Trainer of Basketball Officials, and I really do believe **THE GAME** should have divorced many of us years ago. ☺ **THE GAME** expects and deserves **honor** and a **respect** for its Rules. Not just sometimes but always. I ask you again the same question that caused a paradigm shift in my career when **PETER WEBB** asked me,

> *"If basketball could speak . . . what would it say about the way you officiate?"*

Would it ask for a divorce? What would your answer be? Think about it, would you be guilty of categorizing Rules into three groups?

1. **Rules We Always Enforce**
2. **Rules We Sometimes Enforce**
3. **Rules We Never Enforce**

Are you always true to your spouse or significant other? Always? Sometimes? Never?

Now I recognize that if you are the only one who always enforces the Rules, as we should, you'll really stand out and perhaps temporarily must defend your position of honor for **THE GAME**. However, now that every fan has a camera and instant replays are common as they seek accuracy, it won't be long until all Officials will replace their personal approaches with accurate rules enforcement. When all Officials are motivated enough to always enforce the Rules as written, then **THE GAME** is seen and understood by the coaches, fans, and *"talking heads"* in a manner that is the same at every game. Again, I repeat, the toughest part of officiating these days is Officials asking,

> *"When is the right time to enforce certain rules of THE GAME?" The answer to this question is not the same answer given by every Official.*

We're talking about a game that is well within in its second century, and we are still discussing *"what is the accurate ruling"* to Block/Charge and Continuous Motion contact.

We have all heard the admonition to ***"Trust Your Partners!"*** That's excellent advice when referring to Mechanics.

Now let's add, ***"Trust the Rules,"*** which are designed to ensure a balance between Defense and Offense, Tall and Short, Big and Small, and Strong and Weak. These Rules are perfectly in place to also ensure that **Both Teams** are considered and leaves no room for **THE GAME** Official to decide *"what matters"* at any point in **THE GAME.**

"Everything Matters." It always does.

When we Officials decide to *"do as we please,"* we will never perform the precise description of our Role as Game Officials, which is to

> *"Monitor the activity and make accurate rulings on that activity."*

When we endeavor to *"decide on our own"* what is accurate, we are already inaccurate. We cannot and must not think that we have the right to officiate the way **we** want to. Allow what **we** want to. Condone what **we** choose. Use substitutes for Rules Enforcement that **we** deem to be *"good for the moment."* Even though it may be a noble effort to *"make the moment better,"* it also is an *"intentional inaccuracy,"* because in every case, **both teams** are **not** being considered.

Honor **THE GAME** and the Rules on which it is built because **THE GAME** is its rules. Embrace this avocation. Accept the identity of a Game Official, who has no right to care if a player violates or fouls. Not caring if a player fouls or violates is the same as **not caring** who wins. Accepting this accurate approach is sure to be an obvious public display of affection toward **THE GAME.** Spouses and

THE GAME really like this. Remember, *"When your spouse ain't happy, nobody's happy."* Staying married to **THE GAME** and being its Guardian is much easier and longer lasting when it is filled with **Respect, Honor, Pride, Dignity, and Love.**

> *Therefore, when we have the opportu-*
> *nity, we should do good to everyone . . .*
> *—Galatians 6:10*

DO THE RIGHT
THING. THEN DO THE
RIGHT THING. THEN
DO THE RIGHT THING. WHY?
BECAUSE IT IS THE
RIGHT THING TO DO.

CHAPTER 26

A Thorough Pregame Conference

"Getting Ready Before Getting on the Court"

To state the obvious, every Basketball Official knows what a Pregame Conference is, and hopefully, all of us also know the importance of always having such a conference before going onto the court. And to further state the unfortunate obvious, Pregame Conferences come in all *"shapes and sizes."*

If we were to ask the Referees to describe their Pregame Conferences, we would hear things like, *"We talk as we're getting dressed and see if anyone has had any strange plays in the last few games."* In addition, we will hear some Referees state that they do not even have a written document that they use as their checklist, as they just get the Crew talking about something that is related to basketball.

> I have known only a few referees who actually *"pregamed"* the crew, with any organized checklist. Most of the time, it was simply a casual comment, as if each crew member was good enough not to waste our time discussing specifics.

Here are some actual quotes from the Referee, which was the extent of many of my brief *"pregames"* during my career:

- *"We have officiated together in the past, so we should be okay."*
- *"You guys got anything you want to talk about?"*
- *"Anybody had any funky plays you want to discuss?"*
- *"Okay guys . . . you know what to do, so let's do it."*
- *"Let's just make sure they don't fight."*
- *"Have either of you had these teams?"*
- *"We know what to do, so let's just discuss the coaches."*
- *"Let's talk about the team tendencies."*
- *"Let's just make sure we keep the good players in **THE GAME** and know which ones are the problem players."*
- *"Stay in your primary, and don't throw any crap in **THE GAME**."*
- *"Let's have fun, and don't call anything you can't explain."*

I have personally experienced every one of the above and others, when the Referee of the Crew allowed us to go onto the court, as individual Officials, instead of **one** crew. These are shameful, and we must not condone such because *"**THE GAME** deserves our best!"* And may we never entertain the notion that we are *"at our best"* if we did not have a thorough Pregame Conference.

As a young entrepreneur back in the 1980s, my business partner and I built a very large insurance business throughout the southeast, with agencies in Savannah, Augusta, Macon, Columbus, Mobile, Muscle Shoals, and Atlanta. Visiting our agencies in those cities by car was so time-consuming that I decided to become an airplane pilot.

Takeoffs and landings at six o'clock in the mornings are awesome, but there was so much more to learn. We studied the weather, learned about the planes, the instruments, how planes fly, etc. I really learned to love it, and my initial solo flight remains one of my biggest *"bucket list thrills"* ever.

It was in my pilot training that I was first introduced to a real *"pregame conference,"* which they called a ***Preflight Inspection***. That's when we walked around the plane to make sure it is airworthy because you never want the plane to *"come down"* until you're ready for a landing. If you knew you are going to be in that plane, I'm sure you would find comfort in knowing that a thorough *Preflight Inspection* had been performed and taken very seriously by the pilot. Thoroughly trained airplane pilots take what they do very seriously and would never even consider omitting the use of the Preflight Checklist.

Actually, there are other checklists that pilots rely on during their flights. In addition to the *"walk-around"* inspection, they have a *"takeoff"* checklist, a *"landing"* checklist, an *"emergency"* checklist, and others.

> **I recall asking my flight instructor, early one morning, when I was excited about getting airborne, *"Since we just did the preflight inspection yesterday morning, do we do it again today? Do we do it every time?"***

His response was classic and one I shall probably never forget. He asked me, *"Raymond, did we crash yesterday?"* I smiled and took it as a rhetorical question, which caused him to ask me again, indicating he wanted a verbal response. So I responded with the obvious good news that *"We did not crash yesterday."* To which he asked, *"If things went so well yesterday . . . why would you want to change anything today?"* A great lesson for us all, wouldn't you agree?

By the way . . . my flight instructor also taught me another very important lesson: Never fly with a pilot who says, *"I **think** we have enough fuel to get there."*

The main support materials that Basketball Officials should have with them at all times are the Rules Book, Case Book, and the Officials' Manual. In addition, Officials should have an updated Pregame Conference Card, which consists of the crucial **checklist** of important items that must be discussed with the Crew before going onto the court. The best Pregame Card I have ever seen is created and updated annually by the International Association of Approved Basketball Officials (IAABO). Each season, the IAABO International Office sends their Pregame Conference Cards to each Board, which then distributes them to their entire staff of Officials.

This card is very thorough and is to be used by every IAABO Official around the world. It has proven to be the ultimate tool that brings the crew together, prior to leaving the dressing area. Many refer to it as *"The Crew's Checklist,"* as if they were pilots performing their **Preflight Inspection.**

The real lesson here is

> **Whether you are flying an airplane or officiating a basket-ball game, *"don't leave anything to chance,"* because we know THE GAME has a better *"chance"* at going well, following a thorough pregame conference.**

A few years ago, in my DI days, when assigned the Referee position in the Crew, I began adding the time of the Pregame Conference to my initial verbal contact with the Crew. I, then, included it again in the e-mail the day before **THE GAME**, as another reminder of its importance.

Here is a look at the suggested communication time line for a high school game assignment. Obvious adjustments are needed for college assignments.

- Arrival Time Is 6:00 p.m.
- Dressed and Groomed by 6:15 p.m.
- Pregame Conference Begins at 6:15 p.m.
- Warm-Up (Jogging and Stretching) Begins at 6:35 p.m.
- On Court at 6:45 p.m.
- Game Time Is 7:00 p.m.

These listed times will further communicate the Referee's attitude toward the importance of the Pregame Conference.

The Pregame Conference is not to be viewed or presented as a training session. It is hoped that each Crew Member is skilled enough to be assigned the contest. However, the Pregame Conference is to be perceived as

- a Checklist,
- a Reminder,
- a Memory Jogger,

- *"Batting Practice,"*
- a Warm-Up Drill, and
- Mental Calisthenics.

Please do not be guilty of even thinking that a Pregame Conference is only for the newer Officials. The Checklist is for all Officials to use all the time, like old and young airplane pilots. It is for all Officials, all the time. Accept it . . . Insist on it . . . Do it . . . *"Join the Team!"*

The Referee conducts the Conference, and there is only one Referee. The Umpires are to listen, be attentive, show interest, observe with a positive body language that makes the Referee know they are interested and they care! Umpires do not talk unless a clarification is needed, because the Referee is the *"quarterback"* and no one talks in the huddle except the *"quarterback."*

In addition, during the Pregame Conference, no one is to be

- Grooming,
- Stretching,
- Going Potty,
- on the Phone,
- Texting, or
- Distracted in Any Way.

One of the main responsibilities of the Referee position is to ensure that the crew is *"ready"* when they leave the dressing room. The entire crew must *"check their mental baggage at the door."* The Pregame Conference helps in getting our minds off business and family issues and on officiating basketball. This is a conference, a strategy meeting, a very important time together.

By the way, always remember to *"P"* five times before going onto the court. By that I mean **PPPPP**, a reminder that **"Proper Preparation Prevents Poor Performance."**

A thorough Pregame Conference prevents anything from happening that hasn't already been discussed. It is still on our desktop, still on the front burner and simmering in our minds. No surprises! This approach is the only professional approach that should be accepted and condoned by all Basketball Officials and their Supervisors.

The *"takeaway"* of this chapter is to make sure you and your fellow Officials, all Officials, take the Pregame Conference very seriously. The results of a thorough Pregame Conference are obvious and easily measured.

- The performance will be more professional.
- There will be excellent communications with everyone involved.
- There will be no surprises.
- The crew will be ready before the toss.
- But the best part is . . .

*"**THE GAME** will take off. It will fly, and it will land, just as it should, without crashing."*

Don't depend on your own wisdom. Respect the Lord and refuse to do wrong.
—Proverbs 3:7, NCV

MONITOR THE ACTIVITY
AND MAKE ACCURATE
RULINGS. THE RULINGS ARE
ONLY ACCURATE WHEN
THEY ARE SUPPORTED BY THE RULES BOOK.
WE CAN'T MAKE ACCURATE
RULINGS IF WE DON'T KNOW THE RULES.

CHAPTER **27**

The Complete Package

"Accuracy With The Proper Performance Without Compromise"

If you have read this book to this point, it should be obvious that there is an overlapping theme from chapter to chapter, and that is certainly by design. The theme is the same as the title of this book: *"Performance Without Compromise."* This book is a *"call for commitment"* by Officials to a **Proper Performance** while making **Consistent, Accurate Rulings**. This should be easy to accomplish if all Officials committed to *"mastering"* the Rules, utilizing the Proper Mechanics, and only using the Approved Signals. Since we all have the same Resource Materials and have for many years, one would think this would have been accomplished years ago.

Another theme on these pages is the continual plea for Game Officials to *"rid their officiating"* of any substitutes for Rules Enforcement, which is abundantly present under the guise of *"preventive officiating," "feel for* **THE GAME***," "game management,"* etc.

We all do not have the same *"feel"* or the same *"management skills,"* but we all do have the same Rules Book and the same Officials' manual.

Want **Consistent, Accurate Rulings**? Want the same **proper performance**? Want the same nonverbal communications? My guess is, you do, and that is a good thing. Unfortunately, many do not. Unfortunately, some still believe each Official should use their own *"personal approach"* to officiating, which has left everyone involved in **THE GAME** wondering how this disregard for the rules was ever condoned in the first place. When those in leadership positions accept the fact that officiating is **not** to be about the Officials but about **THE GAME** and the enforcement of its rules, then the illusive *"consistency in officiating"* can be realized, and it won't take a decade to reach this goal.

There is a common denominator in *"officiating excellence,"* and it not only pertains to **Accuracy**, but it is saturated with the required **Proper Performance**, which only occurs when the Official demonstrates competence by using the **Proper Mechanics** and the **Approved Signals**. The Judge in the court room in a liability case always wants to know, *"What does the Rules Book say?"* The Judge never inquires as to what the Officials *"thought or felt"* or what the score was or the time on the clock. We need Assignors and Supervisors to ask similar questions regarding Rules Enforcement while insisting on the use of **Proper Mechanics** and **Approved Signals**.

We have gotten comfortable with the imitation and with customized officiating. We have accepted a hybrid, along with cliché officiating and rhetoric training. The performance level should not rise and fall with roller coaster irregularity, because **THE GAME** is not ours to mess with. However, it is ours to Honor and Respect. When we look beyond the style to the very heart of **THE GAME**, we can easily realize the genuine is still here.

Stop putting the genuine aside and choosing the imitation. THE GAME is calling us back to *"The Basketball Way."*

"The Basketball Way" is the right way, the Rules Book way, and the only way we as a group can reach the goal of **Consistent, Accurate Rulings**. The accuracy of the Official's ruling will always be the same. The ruling is based on the Rules, and the application of

the Rules is not to change due to **THE GAME** situation. The Rules pertaining to Traveling are the same for the fourth quarter as for the first. This same logic applies to all Rules. We Officials must discontinue treating the Rules as a cafeteria line, where we pick and choose to enforce the ones **we** like and disregard or ignore the ones **we** don't.

My hope here has been to *"find the right words"* to motivate us all to develop and appetite for accuracy while pursuing *"**Excellence in Officiating.**"* Excellence can never occur unless we first commit to **Accuracy**, and **Accuracy Is Not Debatable**. Everything must align itself with the Rules Book, Case Book, and Officials' Manual. Once an Official has a commitment to accuracy, then anything that stands between the Official and the commitment will diminish, leave, and go away. It all starts with our training programs, and too much of what has been taught is not rule based. Instead, Officials are being taught a philosophy, a feel, some unique approach, and even that it is okay for Officials to have different judgments. Remember, accurate rulings are only accurate because there is Rules Support for the Ruling.

When we do what is right, long enough, what is wrong will vanish.

Here's our opportunity to change our ways and do things right. There is a right way. There is a standard, and we are not measuring up to it, because of a *"that doesn't matter"* attitude. An attitude that says, *"The main thing is to get the call right."* That attitude is not appropriate at any level and will vanish when **THE GAME** becomes the number one priority. The good news is this: When we put **THE GAME** first, it clearly becomes so much easier to *"get the call right."* By the way . . . many of the Officials with the *"wrong attitude"* of *"just get the call right"* don't do that either. Some of the Officials who pass the *"eye test"* and look good on the court are constantly *"butchering"* Block/Charge, Continuous Motion and Traveling while continuing to advance through the ranks, as the Supervisor continues saying, *"**Well, that's his judgment.**"* The interpretation of this Supervisor's

RAYMOND McCLURE

remark is, *"I really don't know if he is right or not. I never was a rules guy, either."*

The *"main thing"* in high school sports is the *"Life Lessons"* the participants learn that will serve them and our communities in a positive way once these student athletes become adults. The rules and the required performance have these *"lifelong lessons"* at the foundation of the purpose of the schools' extracurricular activities.

> **When we Officials do anything that is contrary to this real purpose, the schools should be filing reports that motivate us to align our performance with that of their mission.**

Obviously, **THE GAME** deserves very skilled Game Officials, but too many assignors/supervisors still think the *"skilled Officials"* are the ones who can *"manage a game"* instead of *"Officiate THE GAME."* As stated elsewhere in this book, *"We are not game managers. We are Game Officials."* Managers manage, and Officials officiate.

We need to change, and it takes a gut-level conviction to challenge the many *"officiating lies"* that have gone unchallenged far too long. To get the needed change, all leaders of Officials need to take a genuine look at where we are as a group, where we've been, and where we're going. Because of **who we are,** we must start measuring the performance of our Officials by comparing their rulings with the expectations of the Rules Book.

> **This can never occur until the leaders themselves become rules experts. Then they will know when their Officials' rulings are accurate.**

Here are some end-of-book reminders:

- Officials are great people—people of integrity and excellent character.
- Officials will follow instructions from the person who assigns their games (should follow the trainer's training).

- Officials are teachable with a desire for accuracy.
- Officials are being taught that accuracy is debatable and often is determined by the situation.
- Officials are taught that accuracy is determined by the ruling Official's judgment.
- Officials are being told that *"everything is fine"* if the coaches don't complain.
- Officials are not being taught to Honor **THE GAME**.
- Officials are being discovered but not developed.
- Officials are judged more on their look and style than the accuracy of their rulings.
- Officials are not to be officiating by a different set of rules than the Rules Book.
- Officials should be remembered for their accuracy, not a style.
- Officials are mocking **THE GAME** when using substitutes for rules enforcement.

It's not just **okay** to know the Rules . . . It's **vital**. It's an **assumption** the Coaches, Media, and Fans **have a right to make**. What other sport comes to mind where Game Officials decide for themselves whether a rule should or should not be enforced? The replay system took care of that in Major League Baseball. What about the Olympics? Should the judging there be of a personal nature? Don't think so. If accuracy were not so important, big-time sports would never have implemented replay rules and expensive replay systems. What about golf? Can you imagine Golf Officials being selected to officiate based on their ability to know **when** not to enforce a rule? Should Golf Officials and Tennis Officials have a *"feel for their game"* so they will know when to rule accurately?

> **Moving forward toward consistent, accurate rulings depends on accountability and accountability begins with expectations.**

We can't fault **THE GAME**, because nearly everything that was legal fifty years ago is still legal. And nearly everything that was illegal fifty years ago is still illegal.

> **The problem is not with the rules; the problem is accepting them and them alone.**

Listen to the rules. Yes! Listen! *"Press your ear against the pages."* Know them like other professionals know their chosen field of excellence. *"Build a fire in your belly"* to do things the right way, all the time.

Officiating is more than passing the *"eye test."* An Official's style cannot be allowed to hide a lack of knowledge. Every Ruling made on the court **Must Be Rule Based.** The Rules have been written to assure us of that. The Rules have been written to *"Make It Easier"* for Officials and leaders to know the ruling was accurate. Again . . . rulings can't go either way. They are only accurate if they have rules support.

I shared this in a previous chapter, but it is certainly worthy of repeating, as it has proven to have a terrible effect on **THE GAME**. It was relayed to me a couple of years ago by an Official who was attending a summer camp, where he heard the ACC Supervisor of Officials instruct the attendees to *"stop calling incidental traveling."* Was the Supervisor really referencing movement that is barely traveling? Or was he insinuating the Officials are ruling traveling violations that aren't there? Either way, there must be better wording when training future and current college Officials.

> **Which floor violations will be next on the list that the Officials will pay big camp fees to be taught not to enforce?**

Is that type of *"training"* going to create group accuracy when making rulings on traveling? We are very familiar with *"Incidental Contact"* because it is rule based. But I have never heard of *"incidental"* traveling, because it is not rule based. Is he instructing his staff to only rule traveling if it is obvious? Seen by everyone? Is he instructing his staff that *"a little bit of traveling"* is acceptable in the ACC? It is *"stuff"* like this that should cause us to hesitate before having certain high-profile leaders as guest speakers or clinicians in our high school training sessions. We need to be providing more than *"incidental training"* so our Officials will never hesitate to make accurate rulings regarding all rules.

> *Have courage enough to face and fight any*
> *opposition to what you know is right.*
> *I have chosen the way of truth.*
> *—Psalm 119:30*

THERE ARE GOOD
SHIPS, AND THERE
ARE BAD SHIPS, BUT THE BEST
SHIPS ARE FRIENDSHIPS.

CHAPTER **28**

My Trip To Maine

"The Way Officiating Ought To Be"

For nearly twenty years, Peter and I have been discussing my coming to Maine to observe their State Basketball Tournament. Knowing Peter as I do, I knew what I would experience, but I sure didn't know all I would witness and appreciate. I had previously promised myself and anyone else who happened to be in the sound of my voice that I would never return to Maine in the winter time. A human being with a Southern accent and below-zero temperatures absolutely do not go together.

I think it was Jacky Loube, former Executive Director of IAABO, who first characterized the home of Peter and Marie as visiting the set from the movie *On Golden Pond*. The description was absolutely *"right on"* as their beautiful log house, log office, and gigantic log garage, with an above apartment, is indeed as peaceful a setting as anywhere to be found. As I type this chapter, I am looking out the huge glass window from the apartment above the garage. I see snow piled up over six feet high by the driveway, firewood perfectly stacked under the front porch, and a five-mile long lake (Pleasant Lake) covered in ice and snow. The giant Black Birds and Blue Birds are constantly putting on a terrific show for me every morning as they pester each other for the crumbs Marie has thrown out onto the snow.

More influence on the rules of basketball at all levels has come from the Log Office, where Peter has spent countless hours writing, reading, responding, and counseling leaders of the NFHS, NCAA, FIBA, and IAABO. When Peter speaks, others are normally listening and realizing they are hearing from the best mind ever in basketball officiating. The usual comments begin with *"I have never thought of it that way."*

This chapter is being created in February 2018. Last Saturday evening, I had a GHSA (Georgia High School Association) first-round assignment for our state tournament at Lithonia High School. My wife, Susie, went with me, and after **THE GAME**, she took me to the Atlanta Airport for my flight to Portland, Maine. My dear friend Barry Fuller picked me up at the airport, and I stayed the night at Echo Farm in Bowdoin, Maine, the childhood home of his wonderful wife Laurie, who is always the perfect Hostess.

The next day, Barry and I, along with nearly one hundred other family and friends of Peter, surprised him for his 80th Birthday at Dysart's Restaurant in Bangor. The show of love and affection for Peter was simply awesome and very difficult to even describe. So not only did I get to surprise Peter, but I got to witness an amazing weeklong State Basketball Tournament that was played in four venues, namely Bangor, Augusta, and two in Portland. Peter is still the Basketball Commissioner for this beautiful state, but he now has three very competent assistants in these three cities; Barry Fuller, TJ Halliday, and David Ames—three native Mainers that I call friends with accents.

Several years previously, Peter called me on a Saturday morning at 8:45 from the old Bangor Auditorium and told me that the two teams that were going to play at 9:00 were from towns of less than 1,200 in population and schools with an enrollment of less than 200 each. What made this interesting was at 8:45 on a very cold and snowy Bangor, Maine, morning, there were already over 5,000 fans in attendance. **WOW!** I knew I wanted to witness such a tournament as soon as I could. Peter's 80th surprise birthday party made it happen, and the tournament was more than I expected, and I knew I wanted to include it in this book for all to read.

Here are some of the things that stood out the most to me and caused me to be tremendously impressed since I have never witnessed any tournament with such attention to detail.

- All games were attended by thousands of fans, not just a few hundred.
- Coaches and their assistants were dressed in business attire and well-groomed.
- Rare to witness a Coach screaming at his/her players.
- Rare to see a Coach receive a Technical Foul.
- Rare to witness unsporting behavior that would warrant a technical foul.
- Opponents assisting opponents up from a fall.
- Players playing hard but never disrespecting their opponents with *"in your face"* body language.
- High School students performed the National Anthem; some singing solo, some duets, and performances from the bands from the participating schools. Awesome renditions of our Country's Anthem.
- Never have I witnessed such reverence during our National Anthem; 5,000 people totally silent when the singer took a breath for the next line to sing. Every time. All venues. No one distracting anyone. Total silence. I was honored to be there, and this alone was worth the trip.
- Full School Bands taking turns to perform during intermissions, which added to the attendance and the stimulation within each venue.
- Officials who were well-groomed, neat, and obviously qualified for the tournament.
- Officials who know the rules and enforce them; no managing, just accurate officiating; no selling, just accurate rulings.
- Game Officials who signaled as instructed by the Rules Book and the Officials' Manual; seen one signal, you've seen them all, all alike.

A serious *"tip of the hat"* to the Maine Principals' Association, the staffs at each of the venues, the table personnel, and the well-behaved fans. It was very obvious that this state is totally aware of the real reason that schools offer sports to their students. The many lessons learned from being involved will assist the participants as they become ex-players and future leaders of their respective communities.

One of Maine's mottos is *"The way life ought to be."* I think I'll give them another one: ***"The way officiating ought to be . . ."***

Consistent, Accurate Rulings and a Performance Without Compromise!

CHAPTER 29

International Association of Approved Basketball Officials

"IAABO Is Still **THE GAME**'s Best Friend."

As the spring was just around the corner and my first basketball officiating season had ended, I found myself even more *"hungry"* to learn. As I've stated, I had just turned thirty-nine when I attended my first Nationwide Referee Camp in Carnesville, Georgia, so I needed to make up for lost time. I wanted to know everything. I really did. As is the case with most of us who had played and/or coached, *"the more I learned, the more I realized how little I actually knew"* on this topic of basketball rules, mechanics, and signals.

That summer, I drove from Atlanta to Washington, DC, to attend a National Referee Convention. It was a long drive but a nice experience. However, it was more about meeting other sports Officials and hearing some fun *"war stories"* and who doesn't like to hear them from Officials we've only met by watching them on the television?

I recall feeling somewhat disappointed, because I was *"hungry"* for knowledge. Again, I needed to collapse the time frames since I was already known as the *"old rookie."* I didn't feel *"old,"* as I could still run with the best of them; but I was seeking someone, some place, some mentor, some organization that trained Basketball Officials.

I would later learn that Charlie Bloodworth was a Past President of the International Association of Approved Basketball Officials (**IAABO**). Most of the college Officials within two hundred miles or so of Atlanta were Members of IAABO Board 13. I would later become President of that Local Board. We met annually at Mary Mac's Restaurant on Ponce de Leon Avenue in downtown Atlanta for our Annual Meeting, and attendance was great, as it was at that dinner meeting our paychecks were dispersed to the local small college Officials.

When I attended by first Annual IAABO Meeting, it only took a few minutes to realize this was the Organization I had been seeking. I was so impressed with the structure of the meetings, the **real** training that was being offered, and I really believed I filled an entire notebook with lots of *"food"* for my *"hungry"* mind.

As I type this, I serve on the International Executive Committee for IAABO, and I really do not believe anyone could be prouder to serve. I do not live in a traditional IAABO locale, but we did our part to bring in over 1,500 new IAABO members about fifteen years ago. However, most of them only stayed members for a year or two, after new leadership for basketball was hired by the Georgia High School Association.

IAABO started in 1921 and is a nonprofit, professional service organization that is for Basketball Officials and is managed by Basketball Officials. Our soon-to-retire Executive Director is Tommy Lopes, a retired high-profile college Basketball Official. He has proven, in my view, to be the best Public Relations Leader in the history of this organization. During his time as Executive Director, we have formed awesome alliances with other major basketball entities. Some of these are NFHS, NASO, NBA, Basketball Hall of Fame, NCAA, USA Basketball, and FIBA. Each of these organizations recognize IAABO as a true leader in Basketball Officiating. IAABO serves its members, other basketball organizations, and **THE GAME** of basketball by providing leadership in all areas pertaining to basketball and basketball officiating.

IAABO CONSTITUTION . . .
ARTICLE II: PURPOSE

The purpose of the Association shall be

1. To educate, train, develop, and provide continuous instruction for basketball Officials;
2. To promote the welfare of **THE GAME** of basketball, its players, and Officials;
3. To maintain the highest standard of basketball officiating;
4. To encourage the spirit of fair play and sportsmanship;
5. To have available at all times an adequate number of thoroughly trained and capable Officials; and
6. To cooperate with all organizations Officially connected with basketball in furthering its interest and ideals.

IAABO Mission Statement

The International Association of Approved Basketball Officials, Inc. is a non-profit and professional organization managed by and for basketball Officials whose primary purpose is to promote, maintain, and insure the welfare of **THE GAME** of basketball and officiating. Through strict development of standards, curricula, and continuous instruction, IAABO trains and educates new and experienced Officials who are duly charged with representing the spirit of fair play, integrity, and sportsmanship. By promoting the principle of "teachable moments," IAABO is dedicated to assisting schools and organizations in achieving their educational goals and furthering the ideals of basketball and officiating.

IAABO is *"sports specific,"* meaning only one sport: **Basketball**, with our motto being, ***"One rule, one interpretation."*** The organization is run by an elected Board of Directors (Executive Committee), representing twelve regions; there are 160 Local Boards in thirty-one States and eight Foreign Countries. We have eight Standing Committees, chaired by Members, who meet twice a year.

IAABO is the oldest, largest, and fastest-growing officiating organization in the world! There really is no other organization like it on the planet, with more than sixteen thousand Basketball Officials as members.

I personally believe that my friend and Mentor **PETER WEBB** was perfectly positioned in IAABO as he served as the International Coordinator of Interpreters (Trainers) for many years (retired in 2017). I also believe him to be the most knowledgeable person ever on the subject of Officiating Basketball Games. Peter is a Past President and Life Member and serves on the NFHS Rules Committee and has participated in the Annual NFHS Rules Committee Meetings for more years than anyone in the history of basketball. His devotion to serving officiating and his commitment to excellence is matchless. He is one of the two individuals to whom I dedicated this book.

DID YOU KNOW?

- **The First NBA Supervisor of Officials Was IAABO Trained.**
- **The NCAA Supervisor of Officials Was IAABO Trained.**
- **The First 6 NCAA Men's Rules Editors Have Been IAABO Trained.**
- **IAABO Trained Officials Dominate the NCAA Tournament.**
- **IAABO Trained Officials Dominate the Final Four.**
- **Eight Out of the Twelve Officials in the Basketball Hall of Fame Are IAABO Members.**

> *"There's no other organization in the world, like IAABO!"*

RECRUITMENT AND TRAINING

- Two Annual International Seminars. FREE Admission to Members
- Regional and Worldwide Officiating Clinics
- Dr. Phil Fox Memorial Clinics . . . Sponsored by the IAABO Foundation
- IAABO Foundation Scholarship Program
- *"Train the Trainers"* . . . Interpreters Clinics

Join us! Only thirty-five dollars per year . . . less than ten cents a day! www.IAABO.org

"IAABO is the best friend __THE GAME__ of basketball has ever had!"

> *Putting confidence in an unreli-*
> *able man is like chewing with a sore*
> *tooth or running on a broken foot.*
> *—Proverbs 25:19*

EXCELLENCE
IS DOING
ORDINARY THINGS
EXTRAORDINARILY WELL.

—John Garner

EXCELLENCE IS NEVER AN ACCIDENT.

CHAPTER 30

Five-Star Basketball Referee Development Program

"Still The Most Thorough Training Experience Anywhere"

The Five-Star Basketball Referee Development Program is designed to create the solid foundation upon which to build a basketball officiating career. It is never too late to build or improve that foundation. We serve as an ongoing resource to Officials and organizations who are dedicated to *"Continuing Education"* and *"Professional Improvement."*

We believe that Basketball Officials are hired to make **Accurate Rulings**. We further believe that the **accuracy** of their rulings can only be determined by comparing them with the Rules Book and Case Book. If there is no Rules Support for the ruling, the Official has *"kicked a rule."* None of our Training Efforts teach a *"philosophical approach"* or some *"unique version"* of officiating basketball games.

We believe Basketball Officials are to **monitor** the activity of everyone involved in **THE GAME** and make **Accurate Rulings** based on what they see and hear.

There are two distinct trainings, which make up the **Five-Star Basketball Referee Development Program:**

1. **The Five-Star Basketball Referee Course (The Course)**
2. **The Five-Star Basketball Referee Camps (The Camps)**

THE COURSE was founded in 1999, and more than 5,200 Officials have attended as of 2017. It has been presented in several states and has proven to far exceed the expectations of all attending Officials, whether they are new to officiating or a seasoned veteran. Much of **THE COURSE** Material is also used at the **Camps**, but much more detailed presentations occur at **THE COURSE.**

Each Official receives our copyrighted sixty-eight-page **Course Workbook**, which serves as the perfect companion for studying the Rules Book and the NFHS Officials Manual; many feel the **Workbook** alone is worth the *"price of admission."*

THE COURSE is a twelve-hour interactive training session that is presented in both the classroom and on the court (no players). All of this is done in an atmosphere that is comfortable, fun, and conducive for learning. The materials are presented in lecture form with visual aids (PowerPoints) and presentations that will be remembered for many years to come, as the passion and enthusiasm become very contagious, even for the veteran Officials. The Officials leave **THE COURSE** inspired, motivated, educated, and passionate about **accuracy** and the **Required Proper Performance.**

The most typical hours of **THE COURSE** are on Saturdays at 9:00–5:00 and Sundays at 1:00–6:00.

THE COURSE has a **100 percent** *"No-Questions-Asked, Money-Back Guarantee."* Specifically *"at 6:01 p.m. on Sunday, any Official who wants their money back receives a complete refund."* They just return **THE COURSE Workbook.** Of all the thousands who have taken **THE COURSE**, **no one** has ever asked for a refund! That fact alone should make all Officials curious enough to want to *"see for yourselves."*

THE CAMPS are usually conducted in June and are **sold out** weeks before scheduled opening day. **THE CAMPS** have players playing, coaches coaching, and Officials officiating, which altogether serves as the perfect setting for Officials to put into practice what has been learned at **THE COURSE.**

Our Clinicians are *"handpicked"* by me and perform their Camp Duties as a **servant**, who is there to **serve** each attending Official in their *"Pursuit of Excellence"* in officiating.

Our Clinicians must be Rules Experts, Basketball Savvy, and *"Care About Others."* In addition, they must believe in and teach *"The Basketball Way."* Not their way, your way, or my way, but *"The Basketball Way."*

The Five-Star Basketball Referee Development Program has been designed to make **THE GAME** better by developing better basketball Officials. *"It is all about THE GAME,"* and Officials are the **True Guardians of THE GAME**. This Program has served thousands of Officials by creating obvious improvement and measurable value while *"collapsing time frames to success."* I do hope you will invite us to prove our value to you by bringing the **Five-Star Basketball Referee COURSE** to your area soon. **THE COURSE Fee** is only $60 per Official (as of 2018), and that includes **THE COURSE Workbook**, which sells on Amazon for $35. (as of 2018).

"Never hesitate to contact me."

RayTheRef@gmail.com
Twitter: @RayTheRef
YouTube: RayTheRef

I will instruct you (says the Lord) and guide you along the best pathway for your life; *I will advise you and watch your progress.*
—*Psalm 32:8*

Whatever your hand finds to do, do it with (all) your might . . .
—*Ecclesiastes 9:10, NKJV*

Below is one of two poems that I share with the Officials on the last day of **THE COURSE**. I have carried this poem with me since it was shared with me in 1974 by a businessman in Columbia, South Carolina. The name of the poem is **THE MAN IN THE GLASS**. Enjoy and allow it to *"speak to you."*

"The Guy in the Glass"

When You Get What You Want in Your Struggle for Wealth,
And the World Makes You King for A Day;
Then Go to the Mirror and Look at Yourself,
and See What That Guy Has to Say.

For It Isn't Your Father or Mother or Wife
Whose Judgment Upon You Must Pass;
The Fellow Whose Verdict Counts Most in Your Life,
Is the Guy Staring Back From the Glass.

He's the Fellow to Please, Never Mind All the Rest,
For He's with You Clear Through to the End,
And You've Passed Your Most Dangerous,
Difficult Test, If the Guy in the Glass Is Your Friend.

You May Be Like Jack Horner and "Chisel" A Plum,
And May Think You're A Wonderful Guy;
But the Man in the Glass Says You're Only A Bum,
If You Can't Look Him Straight in the Eye.

You Can Fool the Whole World Down the Pathway of Years,
And Get Pats on the Back As You Pass;
But Your Final Reward Will Be Heartache and Tears,
If You Cheated the Guy in the Glass.

**COMMIT YOURSELF TO EXCELLING AT
EXCELLENCE! DO THE RIGHT
THING THE RIGHT WAY!**

CHAPTER 31

The Takeaway

"What You Were to Receive from These Pages."

CHAPTER 1: *"Accept Your New Identity"*

Immediately following the Introduction, where we explained the *"real reasons"* for this writing, I shared with you one of the first lessons **PETER WEBB** taught me: **Accept Your New Identity**. Take pride in no longer sounding like a player, coach, or fan, and begin speaking like a Game Official who uses the language of the Rules Book.

CHAPTER 2: *"Guardians of THE GAME"*

THE GAME needs Guardians, more Guardians, real Guardians. Guardians guard. Guardians protect. Guardians care about **THE GAME** and are not swayed or influenced by anything that is contrary to the rules of **THE GAME**, because **THE GAME** is its rules. The Officials Code of Conduct and the rules leave **THE GAME** Officials with no option when it comes to rules enforcement. Real Guardians are easy to identify, as they enforce the rules while officiating with the proper performance and never *"beckon"* substitutes for rules enforcement onto the court.

CHAPTER 3: *"THE GAME Is Its Rules"*

Every game has rules, and the rules are **THE GAME**. What happened to us? Who was the first Official to set aside a rule because of the way he/she felt about the score or the remaining time on the clock or the player with the ball? Stop looking for things to replace the rules, such as Common Sense, *"Feel for **THE GAME**,"* Controlling **THE GAME**, Management Techniques, Philosophies, etc. Simply know the rules, accept them, and enforce them.

CHAPTER 4: *"Four Training Topics to Learn First"*

Before learning how to recognize the pivot foot or learning the guarding rules, there are **Four Training Topics** that every Official should be taught: (1) Why Schools Offer Basketball, (2) **THE GAME** Is What Matters, (3) the Real Role of High School Game Officials, and (4) the Importance of Rules and Rules Enforcement. Each of these is presented in their respective chapters.

CHAPTER 5: *"The Role of High School Basketball Officials"*

This chapter clearly and accurately describes in detail the true Role of Game Officials. In one simple sentence, this is it: *"Monitor the activity and make accurate rulings based on that activity."* This cannot be done unless the Official knows the rules and enforces the rules. Other approaches can be used, but those *"approaches"* are all *"substitutes"* for the required proper performance and for rules enforcement. Accepting this real role is key to the much-needed paradigm shift, like the one I experienced when **PETER WEBB** asked me, *"If **THE GAME** could speak, what would it say about the way you officiate?"*

CHAPTER 6: *"The Real Big League"*

Officials are to officiate **THE GAME** based upon the rules and allow the rules writers who are representing the high schools to determine what rules are best for the purposes of including basketball within schools. Schoolboys and schoolgirls don't play basketball for pictures of dead Presidents (money).

CHAPTER 7: *"Attention State Associations/Leaders of Officials"*

This is probably the most important chapter in this book, as it is directed to those who have the power and authority to implement the rules-based and manual-based directives of this book. Not only the State Leaders but Supervisors, Assignors, and Trainers must *"buy into"* doing whatever it takes to get their Officials to make consistent, accurate rulings, rid **THE GAME** of all substitutes for rules enforcement, and do so with the required proper performance. This game is over 125 years old, and we should not still be discussing what is legal activity and what is not.

CHAPTER 8: *"NFHS Officials Quarterly, 2001 Article"*

Officials do not have to choose between Accurate Rulings and Approved Signals, between Proper Mechanics and rules enforcement. Our commitment to the local community and school is to know and enforce the rules of **THE GAME** but also to perform our other duties without compromising our true role as a Game Official. When we accept education-based officiating assignments, we are committing to serve the school in a manner that assists them in their overall purpose for offering sports to the students.

CHAPTER 9: *"NFHS Officials Quarterly, 2004 Article"*

Too much of the *"training"* we were seeing in summer camps and too much of the magazine articles we were reading were simply a clinician's or writer's personal approach, personal philosophy, or *"how I would do it,"* or *"how we do it back home in our state."* In other words, these noble efforts to train without an emphasis on knowing and enforcing the rules of **THE GAME** were causing Officials to spend more time **learning to prevent** than **learning to enforce.** In other words, more Officials were being trained to be *"game managers"* than were being trained to be On-Court Game Officials.

CHAPTER 10: *"Officials Are Not Game Managers"*

Nowhere among our Rules Book, Case Book, or Officials' Manual can we Officials find instructions to be managers of the basketball game. It is not our role. Management skills vary, just like personal tolerance levels, personal judgment, personal interpretations, etc. One of the biggest and most damaging substitutes for rules enforcement is the term *game management*. **Consistent, Accurate Rulings** cannot be attained when Officials are instructed to use their personal management skills. The real role of high school basketball Officials is clearly described in our support books and in chapter 5.

CHAPTER 11: *"Substitutes for Rules Enforcement"*

The overlapping theme of each chapter is the culprit of using and the condoning of *"substitutes for rules enforcement."* Video replay at the college and pro levels of play is not checking to see if the Officials used excellent management skills, controlling techniques, or whether the Official had a good *"call selection"* to keep the star player in **THE GAME**. No. Never. The replay system has been implemented to ensure and double-check to see if the Official's ruling was accurate based on the **RULES OF THE GAME**. No Official wants to *"kick a rule,"* but anytime a substitute for rules enforcement is used, that is exactly what they are doing. Regardless of what other category the Official uses to defend his/her decision not to enforce, it is still *"kicking a rule."*

CHAPTER 12: *"Signals Are the Language of THE GAME."*

Signaling really is the nonverbal language of **THE GAME** Officials. Signals and signaling have deteriorated to such a level that it is rare to find any two Game Officials signaling the same way on any whistle. Some Officials really do try, while others have an attitude that constantly says, *"The main thing is to get the 'call' right."* The culprit in this lack of proper performance regarding signals and signaling is the lack of accountability by the Trainers, Assignors, and Supervisors. Nothing will change in this area until those leaders hold their Officials accountable for their signaling, as much as they do for mechanics. Remember . . . Signals and Mechanics are not the same.

CHAPTER 13: *"Philosophers in the Gym"*

Nearly every officiating book purchased has a chapter or much reference to a *"philosophy"* of officiating. How any organization could *"anoint themselves with the power"* to have their own *"philosophy"* to officiating has proven to be one of the biggest *"shocks"* in my officiating career. I hope I live long enough to stop seeing that word in print because **"nothing Officials do is ever to be philosophical! Never!"**

CHAPTER 14: *"No Calls Are a Myth."*

We must begin teaching Officials at all levels that Game Officials are to enforce the **rules**. We do that by making **rulings** on the activity we monitor. Since nearly everything players do is legal, nearly every **ruling** we make is without the use of a whistle. In other words, Game Officials make *"thousands upon thousands"* of **rulings** during a game, and sometimes they need a whistle. When the **ruling** is legal activity, no whistle is needed; illegal activity requires the use of a whistle. When we think and teach this way, it is easy to see that *"no calls"* and *"I passed on it"* are an absolute myth. We never have a *"no call,"* and we never *"pass on anything."* We are simply **ruling** the activity to either be legal (no whistle) or illegal (whistle). I truly believe this is a better description of what Game Officials actually do while officiating. Please buy into this and spread the word.

CHAPTER 15: *"Basketball Officials Can't Have Their Own Strike Zone."*

Often, we hear comments about the baseball or softball umpire's strike zone, his strike zone or her strike zone. Our friends who officiate behind the plate should be reminded that the Baseball/Softball Rules Books clearly define what a strike is and what it is not. When a pitched ball is called a strike and the pitch was not in the strike zone, the Umpire has *"kicked a written rule"* of their sport. Plate Umpires, at higher skill levels of play, are now being held accountable for the accuracy of the balls and strikes they call. Again, inaccurate rulings cannot be condoned due to the Official's personal judgment. This book is about basketball officiating and basketball Officials' rulings are either accurate or inaccurate based on the written word of our Rules Book and not an Official's personal *"strike zone."*

CHAPTER 16: *"Contact Is Also Rules Based."*

Since the Rules Book is very clear as to what contact is legal and what is not legal, no personal interpretations are needed. Violations are to be officiated by the rules, and so is contact. When Officials master the difference between legal and illegal contact (incidental versus foul), their rulings will begin to be predictable from one court to the other—one game to the other; one Official to the other. Don't you think it is about time, since **THE GAME** is now more than 125 years old?

CHAPTER 17: *"Stop Talking and Officiate."*

One of the strongest debates we often hear is Officials sharing how good they are at *"preventive officiating."* I was certainly raised on that approach, but once I was really trained on the subject, I stopped talking and enforced the rules. I really hope you'll buy into and discontinue the *"talking nonsense,"* which often is a substitute for rules enforcement. Our role is not to prevent but to enforce. This role is much easier to accept when we stop caring if they foul or violate.

CHAPTER 18: *"Enough with the 'Selling' Already."*

"Selling our rulings" is an effort to convince others that *"we got it right."* By the way, no amount of *"selling"* makes a ruling accurate. It is accurate or inaccurate, based on the written word. We never want to appear unsure, but when our signaling loses its dignity and composure and doesn't resemble the diagrams in the Signals Chart, we are proving to be more concerned with *"what others think"* than with the required **Proper Performance**.

CHAPTER 19: *"Always Consider Both Teams."*

Officials must realize that every ruling we make has an effect on both teams—always good for one and always *"not so good"* for the other. There are always two teams to consider. When the Official considers both teams, then the Official stops caring if either team fouls or violates and stops caring if either team wants the clock stopped or doesn't want it to stop. Noble efforts to prevent a three-seconds violation favors Team A over Team B. Having a tolerance for hand checking by telling B1 to *"get your hands off"* always favors Team B. A1 should ask the monitoring Official if he *"has any tips for him."* Considering both teams makes officiating much easier and removes all appearances of favoritism. Hopefully, this chapter causes us all to realize that enforcing the rules never unfairly affects either team.

CHAPTER 20: *"Every Game Has an Ending."*

As **THE GAME** is approaching the end, often the team that's losing will have to make some changes in their efforts to overcome the team that's winning. Conversely, the team that's winning may also have to incorporate some adjustments and strategies to keep their lead and eventually win the contest. On the other hand, Game Officials cannot get caught up in what the Head Coaches are doing. We may anticipate and even know what they both must do, but none of these adjustments should have any effect on us, because our Role remains the same. Our Role does not change. Our rulings are to remain the same, regardless of the score, the time on the clock, or the number of fouls on the star player.

CHAPTER 21: *"Ticky-Tack Fouls"*

This chapter is very clear that *"ticky-tack"* is another myth, and we should call it what it is. It is more than a slang term, because the contact is either a foul or incidental. Either an accurate ruling or an inaccurate ruling. Contact that is a foul is always a foul, and contact that is incidental is always incidental. When an Official rules a foul for contact that is clearly incidental and have been incidental earlier in **THE GAME**, then that is not a *"ticky-tack"* foul; it is an inaccurate ruling, a *"kicked rule."*

CHAPTER 22: *"Don't Forget to Learn the Last Rule."*

It has become painfully obvious that many Officials from local high school games to college games are simply not experts on the rules pertaining to Contact. If they were, we wouldn't continue to see block/charge and continuous motion rulings with no rules support. Officials must master Rules 4.23, 4.11, 4.24, and 4.27, as well as the last two and a half pages of the NFHS Rules Book.

CHAPTER 23: *"Natural-Born Basketball Official?"*

This chapter refutes the notion that some Officials are *"natural-born"* game Officials. Some Officials may be a naturally faster runner or have quicker reflexes than others, just as players do. However, just as there are no *"natural-born"* doctors or plumbers, there are no *"natural-born"* Game Officials. They must learn the skill. They must be trained. They must learn the rules. They must have very good eyesight, etc. They may die a doctor, a plumber, or a Game Official; but they were born a baby. Somewhere in the dash on their tombstone they got trained.

CHAPTER 24: *"The Rules of the Road"*

Driving a vehicle is also a learned skill. Like Game Officials, the driver must have excellent eyesight. In addition, there is a required proper performance when getting behind the wheel of a two-ton bullet and *"shooting it down the highway."* That performance is governed by the Rules of the Road. If the main thing is to get to the destination, then if you arrive without an accident, you are successful, and how you got there doesn't matter. You could run red lights, roll through stop signs, nearly hit pedestrians, turn into wrong lanes, never signal, exceed the speed limits, etc. None of these matter if you reach your goal, which is to arrive at your destination. Now parallel that thinking to officiating a basketball game. If your attitude is one that says, *"Just get the call right,"* then your performance on the court doesn't matter to you, but believe me, it matters to **THE GAME**. In fact, when we are on the court, *"Everything Matters!"*

CHAPTER 25: *"For Better or Worse"*

You quickly could see that I'm not a marriage counselor, but you also learned that many of us should have been divorced by **THE GAME** years ago because of the way we treat it.

CHAPTER 26: *"A Thorough Pregame Conference"*

The purpose here is to convince all readers that they are *"never at their best"* when they go onto the court without being involved in a thorough pregame conference. **PPPPP, the Five Ps** will help you.

CHAPTER 27: *"The Complete Package"*

Even though the theme and lessons often overlap intentionally, this chapter pulls it all together and, hopefully, also pull each reader onto the Team that works very hard to make Consistent, Accurate Rulings with the Proper Performance.

CHAPTER 28: *"My Trip to Maine"*

February 2018 will long be remembered, as I got to visit with **PETER WEBB** for his surprise 80th birthday party and attend the state of Maine's High School Basketball Tournament. Peter's wife, Marie, and his daughter, Elizabeth, pulled off the ultimate surprise for Peter, and the tournament was all I expected and more. It was tremendously refreshing to witness Basketball Officials all signaling the same way, as instructed by the Signals Chart, and judging accurately on block/charge, continuous motion, and traveling. It was as if they had already read *Performance Without Compromise.* Thank you, **PETER WEBB,** for holding the Maine Officials accountable for the accuracy of their rulings and their on-court performance.

CHAPTER 29: *"International Association of Approved Basketball Officials"*

Simply put, *"IAABO is the greatest basketball officiating organization in the world,"* the only remaining true Guardian of **THE GAME**. There is no other organization like it anywhere. The Basketball organization **for** Basketball Officials that is run **by** Basketball Officials. IAABO has been and still is *"the best friend THE GAME has ever had."* This chapter is a must-read because **you should be a member.**

CHAPTER 30: *"The Five-Star Basketball Referee Course"*

The more I got trained by **PETER WEBB**, the more I realized that I wanted to teach others what he taught to me. I have been doing so now since 1999. **THE COURSE** is very like the New Official Training by most IAABO boards. However, it is taught on Saturdays at 9:00–5:00 and on Sundays at 1:00–6:00. This really is the best two-day training session ever created and presented. This is a **Course** where we have lots of edutainment (fun learning). Each attendee receives our first book, which is the Course Workbook that parallels the NFHS Rules Book and NFHS Officials Manual. We bring **THE COURSE** to you and your Officials.

CHAPTER 31: *"The Takeaway"*

You just finished chapter 31. It would be wise to carry this book with you at all times so you can often review chapter 31, as it is the main *"takeaway"* from each chapter. When you share this information with other Officials and/or Coaches, rest assured that you are only sharing what is *"The Basketball Way,"* the *"Right Way,"* as defined and described in the Rules Book, Case Book, and the NFHS Officials Manual. Most of the material in this book also applies to college basketball; if not, I strongly believe it should. But be reminded once again high school sports are offered to students for the many lifelong lessons that can and should be learned from participating—lessons that can't be learned in the *"other"* classrooms. Yes, the gym in high school basketball is an extension of the classroom, so schoolboy and schoolgirl basketball should always be education based.

CHAPTER 32: *"Final Commentary"*

Keep your priorities in the correct order: Faith, Family, Occupation, Officiating. Life is about choices, so choose wisely.

"First, They <u>IGNORE</u> You . . .
Then, They <u>LAUGH</u> at You . . .
Then They <u>FIGHT</u> You . . .
THEN, YOU WIN."

—Gandhi

CHAPTER **32**

Final Commentary

"Keep Your Priorities in the Correct Order."

Over the last thirty plus years, I have witnessed several divorces by Basketball Officials; some of which were very close friends. *"Falling in love"* with officiating can be an easy way to allow it to be wrongfully placed in our list of priorities. I wholeheartedly believe in *"pouring yourself into your efforts"* but not at the expense of more important commitments. In our training Camps and the Five-Star Course, my closing remarks always include *"keeping your priorities in the right order."* When we don't, we are setting ourselves up for a *"rough-road marriage"* or a serious distraction from our Faith and life values.

Our suggested order of priorities is
FAITH, FAMILY, OCCUPATION, OFFICIATING
As we say often,

> *"Life is about choices. First, you make the choices, and then the choices make you."*

I encourage you to choose your priorities wisely.

My dear friend and Rules Expert Paul Behr, from South Carolina, by way of New Jersey, created a **Thank-You Card** the size of a business card with remarks on both sides. I was so impressed with it, I included it here. One side says, *"Thank You for Your Service and Dedication to THE GAME of Basketball."* *The* other side reminds us that we Officials are unsung Heroes where it reads, **UNSUNG HEROES,** followed by, *"There are few who applaud what you do. However, without you, the many lessons that young people glean from their participation in THE GAME of basketball would not be possible. Please accept this simple card as a small token of appreciation."*

Those of you in leadership positions may want to take advantage of this very worthwhile appreciation idea by having such cards created and given to your staff of Officials.

Thank you for reading *Performance Without Compromise.* Because of the way many of us have been *"raised in officiating,"* you may find it most difficult to comply with the directions found in each chapter. However, I remind you again: **The Right Way to officiate is rule based and manual based.** Nothing is to be *"my way"* or *"your way,"* but **THE** way. **THE** right way, and there is a right way. **THE** way has no substitutes for rules enforcement, no personal tolerance levels, no philosophies, no personal interpretations, no unique feel, no unique management skills, etc. In other words, we believe that a commitment to **Consistent, Accurate Rulings** while using the **Proper Mechanics** mandated by your state or conference and the **Approved Signals** for **THE GAME** you are officiating is the very best way for any game of basketball to be officiated. Plus, excellent people skills and communication skills are an absolute must.

> *"Never let your failures go to your heart or your success go to your head."*

Thank you, **PETER WEBB**, for all you mean to me and to basketball officiating and the many wonderful contributions you have made over the last fifty plus years. Thank you for reminding us that we should *"care about everything, because everything matters."* Thanks also for teaching thousands and thousands of Officials worldwide to

- be thorough about everything,
- care about everything,
- always remain composed,
- be dignified,
- be professional in all we do,
- use Rules Book terminology, and
- honor THE GAME we're officiating.

PETER WEBB, you truly are *"the best friend THE GAME of basketball has ever had."* My life and my officiating are so much better because our paths crossed, thanks to IAABO, many years ago.

The most important conclusion I gleaned from Mr. Webb was that of my individual responsibility to . . . THE GAME.

Learn the truth and never reject it. Get
wisdom, self-control and understanding.
                        —Proverbs 23:23, NCV

WATCH YOUR ACTIONS, THEY BECOME HABITS.
WATCH YOUR HABITS,
THEY BECOME CHARACTER.
WATCH YOUR CHARACTER, IT WILL
BECOME YOUR DESTINY.

If you are one of the many thousands of Officials who have attended our Camps or our Courses over the last many years, you'll recall my reading the below poem at our last classroom session. It is always my prayer that you know how much I sincerely care about all Officials and officiating. May God bless you always, and I do mean you.

*****

"Did I Help or Hurt Today, Lord?"

Is any soul happier because I passed this way?
Does anyone remember that I spoke to them today?

When the time is over and toiling time is through,
Will anybody utter a kind word for me to You?

I wonder can I say tonight, in passing
With a day that's slipping fast,
Did I help a single person of the many that I passed?

Is a single heart rejoicing over what I did or said?
Does anyone whose hope was fading, now with hope look ahead?

Did I waste this day or did I lose it;
Was it well or poorly spent?
Did I leave A trail of kindness
Or a scar of discontent?

And as I close my eyes in slumber,
With all my heart I'll pray,
That God above will say I've earned one more tomorrow,
By the speech I gave today.

—Herb True

Beginnings and Endings

Below is one of the best Study Guides ever created. We have many others that have proven to be a terrific source for easy-learning of the rules. Each Study Guide is very thorough and presented in the proper sequence to make learning so much easier. The below document is the best example of how **PETER WEBB** thinks, trains, and mentors. There is no requirement for the Official to memorize the location of the rules references of each activity, but rather to simply know **when** the activity Officially begins and **when** it ends. Game Officials must *"master"* the rules pertaining to the *"Beginnings & Endings"* of each situation listed. Read it often. Request a PDF copy of this 8-page document and/or others by emailing the author at **RayTheRef@gmail.com.**

"BEGINNINGS AND ENDINGS"
BRIEFING FOR NEW OFFICIALS &
REVIEW FOR VETERANS

"ACT OF SHOOTING"/TRY FOR GOAL/TAP
(RULE 4.41.1–8)

BEGINS
- TRY FOR GOAL . . . When the player begins the motion which habitually precedes the release of the ball
- TAP . . . When the player's hand touches the ball

ENDS
- When the throw is successful
- When it is certain the throw is unsuccessful
- When the thrown ball touches the floor
- When the ball becomes dead

AIRBORNE SHOOTER
(RULE 4.1)

BEGINS

- After airborne player releases the ball for a try for goal
  - All airborne shooters were first an airborne player.

ENDS
- When one foot is returned to the floor

ARRIVAL AT GAME SITE

BEGINS
- Not later than one hour prior to game time

CAREER

BEGINS
- Under the guidance of a well-prepared interpreter/trainer

ENDS
- Start by taking an honest look in the mirror.

CLOSELY GUARDED
(RULE 4.10)

BEGINS
- When the defender is initially in legal guarding position within six feet of player who is in control of the ball (holding or dribbling)
- Continues as long as the defender is within six feet of player who is in control of the ball
  - No particular guarding stance or movement is required
  - May involve more than one defensive player

ENDS
- When the defender is no longer within six feet
- When the defender is *"beaten"* (head and shoulders past the defender)
- During an interrupted dribble
- When the player being guarded loses control of the ball

CONTINUOUS MOTION
(RULE 4.11)

BEGINS
- When the habitual throwing motion starts a try or with the touching of the ball on a tip/tap

ENDS
- When the try, tap is clearly in flight
  - Applies only if the foul is committed by an opponent
  - May complete any legal arm, foot, or body movement
  - Applies . . . if beginning is prior to a foul occurring
  - Applies . . . if a teammate is fouled
  - Does not apply if a teammate commits a foul prior to release of ball
  - Expiration of time

CONTROL, PLAYER
(RULE 4.12.1)

BEGINS
- When a player holds or dribbles a live ball
- Includes free throw and throw-in (when the ball is available or at the disposal)

ENDS
- When the ball is released on a pass, try
- During an interrupted dribble
- During a fumble
- When the ball becomes dead (exception—airborne shooter)
- When the opponent secures control

NOTE
- In other words: *"When a player is no longer holding or dribbling a live ball."*

CONTROL, TEAM
(RULE 4.12.2–3)

BEGINS
- When a player has control

ENDS

- When the ball is released on a try, tap
- When an opponent secures control
- When the ball becomes dead

COUNTING SITUATIONS

Rule 4.10, 4.42.3 and 4, 9.10.1a (Closely guarded)
Rule 8.4, 9.1.3a (Free throw)
Rule 9.2 and 4 (Throw-in)
Rule 9.7 3 (Three seconds)
Rule 9.8 (Backcourt)

BEGINS

- Closely guarded . . . when the defender is within six feet of the player in control of the ball
- Free throw . . . when the ball is at the disposal of the free thrower
- Throw-in . . . when the ball is at the disposal of the thrower-in
- Three-seconds . . . when an offensive player enters the lane after team control is established in the frontcourt
- Backcourt . . . with player control

ENDS

- Closely guarded
  - When the defender is no longer within six feet
  - Offensive player no longer has the ball
  - Offensive player *"beats"* defender
  - Ball becomes dead
- Free throw
  - When the free thrower releases the ball
- Throw-in
  - When the thrower-in releases the ball
- Three seconds
  - When an offensive player leaves the lane

- ▪ Suspend count for A1 to complete movement to try for goal
- Backcourt
  - o When the ball has frontcourt status

CONTINUOUS EDUCATION AND PROFESSIONAL IMPROVEMENT

<u>BEGINS</u>
- With a devoted, energized, knowledgeable, and professional interpreter/trainer
- Registration with a local IAABO Board

<u>ENDS</u>
- Never ending

DEAD BALL
(RULE 6.7)

<u>BEGINS</u>
- When a goal is scored, foul, violation . . . and others (See rule 6.7)

<u>ENDS</u>
- When the ball becomes live during a jump ball, free throw, throw-in

DISQUALIFIED PLAYER
(RULE 4.14.1–2)

<u>BEGINS</u>
- As soon as the head coach is notified

<u>ENDS</u>
- When the interval of time ends

DRIBBLE
(RULE 4.15.3 AND 4A, B, C, D, E)

BEGINS
- When a player pushes, throws, or bats the ball to the floor before the pivot foot is lifted

ENDS
- When the dribbler catches or causes the ball to come to rest in one or both hands
- When the dribbler simultaneously touches the ball with both hands
- When the ball touches or is touched by an opponent and causes the dribbler to lose control
- When the ball becomes dead

NOTE
- A player can never travel while dribbling.

DRIBBLE, INTERRUPTED
(RULE 4.15.5–6)

- When the ball is loose after deflecting off the dribbler
- When the ball momentarily gets away from the dribbler

ENDS
- When the dribbler regains control by holding
- When the dribbler continues to dribble

FREE THROW
(RULE 4.20.2–3; RULE 4.8)

- When the ball is at the disposal of the free thrower

ENDS

- When the try is successful
- When certain try will not be successful
- When try touches the floor or any player
- When the ball becomes dead

NOTES

- One and one BEGINS on the seventh team foul of each half
- Two shot penalty BEGINS on tenth foul of each half

FUMBLE
(RULE 4.21)

BEGINS

- When the ball unintentionally drops, slips from a player's grasp

ENDS

- When the player catches the ball
- When the player converts the fumble (when possible) into a dribble

GAME
(RULE 4.28.1; 5.6.1–2, EXCEPTION: 6.1)

BEGINS

- When the ball becomes live for the first time

ENDS

- When the horn sounds/LED light illuminates, unless ball in flight on try for goal

GOALTENDING
(RULE 4.22)

BEGINS

- When the ball is touched on downward flight

GUARDING
(RULE 4.23.1, 2, 3)

BEGINS

- When a player obtains legal guarding position

ENDS

- When the player is legally "beaten" (head and shoulders past)

HELD BALL
(RULE 4.25)

BEGINS

- When opponents have their hands so firmly on the ball that individual player control cannot be obtained without undue roughness
- An opponent places his/her hand(s) on the ball and prevents an airborne player from throwing the ball or releasing the ball on a try for goal

ENDS

- When the whistle sounds

INTERMISSION
(RULE 5.5.1; 2.12.4)

BEGINS

- When a quarter ends

ENDS
- When time expires for the intermission between quarters and half time

INTERVAL OF TIME
(RULE 2.12.5)

BEGINS
- When the Official instructs the timer to start the timing device

ENDS
- When the purpose of stopping play has been resolved
- When the signal to resume play (second signal) sounds

JUMP BALL
(RULE 4.28.3)

BEGINS
- When the ball leaves the Official's hand(s)

ENDS
- When the touched ball contacts a nonjumper, the floor, a basket, or backboard

LIVE BALL
(RULE 6.1; 6.7)

BEGINS
- Jump ball . . . when the ball leaves the Official's hand(s)
- Throw-in . . . when the ball is at the disposal of thrower-in
- Free throw . . . when the ball is at the disposal of free thrower

ENDS

- When the ball becomes dead, as in
  - foul, violation, quarter/extra period ends, inadvertent whistle, time-out, held ball, other whistle (i.e. Blood, injury)

OFFICIALS' JURISDICTION
(RULE 2.2.2)

BEGINS

- When the Officials arrive on the floor

ENDS

- When he/she is beckoned into **THE GAME** by an Official or becomes a player

THREE SECONDS
(RULE 9.7)

BEGINS

- When all of the following are present
  - Front court team control
  - Team a player in the lane (with or without the ball)

ENDS

- When team control ends
- When team a player leaves the lane

UNIQUENESS OF COUNT

- Suspend count when A1 is trying for goal
- Nonvisible

THROW-IN
(RULE 4.42.3–4)

BEGINS
- When the ball is at the disposal of the thrower-in

ENDS
- When passed ball touches or is legally touched by another player inbounds
- When passed ball touches or is touched by another player out of bounds (ex. 7.5.7)
- When the throw-in team commits a violation

NOTE
- The AP Arrow is switched when the throw in ends

TYPES OF THROW-IN
- Designated spot throw-in
- Following successful goal
- AP throw-in

BEGINS
- When the Official instructs the timer to start the timing device

ENDS
- When the signal to resume play (second signal) sounds

QUARTER & EXTRA PERIODS
(RULE 4.5.6.1–2, EXCEPTION: 5.7)

BEGINS
- When the ball first becomes live

ENDS

- When the horn sounds/LED Lights illuminates
  - Exceptions
    - o Ball in flight during try, tap
    - o Held ball or violations occurs so near expiration of time
    - o Foul occurs so near the expiration of time and free throws are involved

---

But if we confess our sins, He will forgive our sins, because we can trust God to do what is right. He will cleanse us from all the wrongs we have done.
—1 John 1:9, NCV

**WE CAN'T MAKE
ACCURATE RULINGS
WITHOUT KNOWING
THE RULES.**

THERE IS NO ACCURACY OUTSIDE THE RULES.

ABOUT THE AUTHOR

Ray McClure officiated Men's DI Basketball for twenty years. In addition, his officiating career has also afforded him the opportunity to officiate in three women's pro leagues, namely the ABL, NWBL, and the WBCBL. A major highlight came in 1996, when he was selected to officiate Scrimmage Games in the 1996 Olympic Games in his hometown of Atlanta, Georgia.

Presently, McClure serves the American Basketball Association (ABA) as a crew chief and rules interpreter for the staff of over four hundred Officials and eighty-plus teams in the United States, Canada, and Mexico. He has traveled for the ABA to Singapore to train the Chinese basketball Officials and officiate the International ABA Team from that area.

Mr. McClure has served on the IAABO Executive Committee and is a frequent presenter and speaker at its annual seminars. He has also served IAABO as an instructor/clinician at its summer schools and has traveled to Germany and Italy for ten consecutive years to train the European Basketball Officials of the United States military.

McClure is an author with published articles in *Referee* magazine, *Officials Quarterly*, and *Sportorials*. RayTheRef, as he is affectionately called, is also the founder of the Five-Star Referee Course. The course workbook has proven to be his most popular publication, to date, as it parallels the Rules Book and Officials manual and serves the Official year after year.

Ray's passion for training basketball Officials is obvious to others, and his goal is to make himself available to assist in this endeavor throughout the world.

Ray lives in Atlanta, Georgia, with his wife, Susie, and is a member of the GHSA and the Peach State High School Basketball Officials Association.

CPSIA information can be obtained
at www.ICGtesting.com
Printed in the USA
BVHW071340150719
553470BV00003B/284/P